# Praise for *Past Present*

"I read *Past Present* at a time when I was eager to understand what patterns from my past still have a negative hold on me now as a senior citizen. With the diagnostic precision you'd expect from an MD, Scott Vaudrey provides remarkable insight and clarity to the complexities of early life, guiding readers on a path toward a healthier today. He takes readers on a journey, employing a set of tools, that will help them identify childhood wounds, reassess those wounds through an adult filter, and step into a new beginning with greater emotional freedom. I benefited tremendously from this book and would highly recommend it to anyone struggling to emerge from the dark storms of their early life. Thank you, Scott, for helping me unlock my past for the benefit of my present."

—Scott Kuethen, CEO, Amtec Human Capital

"This book is for anyone who wants to understand themselves at a deeper level. Tremendously well-written, *Past Present* took a hold of me from the first chapter to the end. Dr. Vaudrey helps you to recognize relational patterns and to look at your past from a new angle. He equips you to make changes that will improve your life today. This book is deeply thoughtful, engaging, and at times piercing. I highly recommend it."

—Thomas Yoon, President, Excelerate Capital

"*Past Present* is an amazing resource! It's the only resource I've found that connects all the dots between my upbringing and my relationships today. Dr. Vaudrey comes at this from three perspectives: medical, seasoned leadership, and personal experience. My wife and I have already had some key conversations over this remarkable content, and I'm buying copies for friends."

—Dr. Terry Franson, Senior Vice President Emeritus, Azusa Pacific University; USA Olympic Track and Field Coach

"What a gift Scott gives to anyone looking for deeper understanding on the origins of psychological pain. Chapter 6 alone should be required reading for anyone in a significant relationship. Leave it to a former emergency room physician to bring clarity and rigor to the process of diagnosing the origins of our emotional suffering. He outlines the science behind our negative reactions and provides effective methods for constructively managing our emotions. *Past Present* integrates the best therapeutic processes with comprehensive research, and Scott adds his own story of healing along with dozens of practical examples of how this process works.

As a psychologist with more than thirty years on the front row of psychological pain and healing, I believe this book offers readers the key to understanding one's core psychological wounds, and a road map for healing and personal growth."

—Andrew Hartman, Psychologist; Senior
Leadership Consultant, NuBrick Partners

"Once again Dr. Vaudrey proves to be a faithful guide. The wisdom and simple, practical tools included in this book helped me make the connection between my messages of past wounds and my story today. While many of us know that our painful memories shaped us in some way, we get stuck ruminating on past experiences or we look to external circumstances to explain our unhappiness. *Past Present* helps you understand the relationship between past hurts and the healthy relationships we all desire, while helping you gain control over the trajectory of your relationships today."

—Sarah Riebe, COO, Slingshot Group

"As a business owner with a relational style of leadership, I care deeply about providing quality leadership to my 500+ employees. When things go wrong at work, it almost always involves a relational breakdown, and quick fixes don't fix anything. In *Past Present*, Vaudrey outlines a laser-clear road map for gaining insight into how I interact with others. As he writes, 'I want to screw up my relationships a little bit less every day.' It's a mindset change. The time you invest in reading this book and using these tools to explore your own relationships will pay huge dividends in your organization, and the payoff will bring real, lasting change—at work and at home."

—Bob McConkey, CEO and President, McConkey Auto Group

# PAST PRESENT

# PAST
# PRESENT

### How to Stop Making the Same Relationship Mistakes—and Start Building a Better Life

## SCOTT VAUDREY, MD

NELSON
BOOKS

An Imprint of Thomas Nelson

*Past Present*

© 2020 Scott Vaudrey

Published in Nashville, Tennessee, by Nelson Books, an imprint of Thomas Nelson. Nelson Books and Thomas Nelson are registered trademarks of HarperCollins Christian Publishing, Inc.

Author is represented by The Christopher Ferebee Agency, www.christopherferebee.com.

Thomas Nelson titles may be purchased in bulk for educational, business, fund-raising, or sales promotional use. For information, please e-mail SpecialMarkets@ThomasNelson.com.

Any Internet addresses, phone numbers, or company or product information printed in this book are offered as a resource and are not intended in any way to be or to imply an endorsement by Thomas Nelson, nor does Thomas Nelson vouch for the existence, content, or services of these sites, phone numbers, companies, or products beyond the life of this book.

ISBN 978-1-4002-1340-5 (audiobook)

**Library of Congress Cataloging-in-Publication Data**

Names: Vaudrey, Scott, author.
Title: Past present : how to stop making the same relationship mistakes--and start building a better life / Scott Vaudrey, MD.
Description: Nashville : Thomas Nelson, [2020] | Includes bibliographical references. | Summary: "Past Present shows readers how to change destructive relationship patterns by identifying the root issues from their pasts and finding the source of healing for their unique stories"--Provided by publisher.
Identifiers: LCCN 2019057324 (print) | LCCN 2019057325 (ebook) | ISBN 9781400213382 (paperback) | ISBN 9781400213399 (ebook)
Subjects: LCSH: Interpersonal relations--Religious aspects--Christianity. | Diaries--Authorship--Psychological aspects.
Classification: LCC BV4597.52 .V375 2020 (print) | LCC BV4597.52 (ebook) | DDC 248.4--dc23
LC record available at https://lccn.loc.gov/2019057324
LC ebook record available at https://lccn.loc.gov/2019057325

*Printed in United States*

20 21 22 23 24  LSC  10 9 8 7 6 5 4 3 2 1

*To my children:*
*Matthew and Andrea,*
*Bethany and Ryan,*
*Katherine,*
*Samuel,*
*September and Scott.*
*My world—and the whole world—are better because of you.*
*I love you,*
*Dad*

We all come by our stories and our interpretation of the world through the lives we've led and particularly through the earliest formative years of our development. Yes, we are capable of adjusting the landscape, and reworking the frameworks, but first we have to see them!

—Pamela McLean, *Self as Coach, Self as Leader*

# Contents

# Contents

# An Invitation to Do the
# Rest of Your Life Better

If I told you there was a way to make your most troublesome relationships better, would you be interested? Most people find this offer intriguing. They'd love to get to the root of a problem and resolve those nagging patterns that sabotage harmony and connection with the people who matter most. However, when I share that the pathway to healthier relationships will require an exploration of their story—their childhood and the family that influenced and shaped them—the less-motivated people suddenly become less interested.

I wish there were an easier path to the life and relationships we all want. There just isn't. And sometimes even the most motivated people struggle to overcome the behaviors that damage their relationships.

I have a friend named Brian. In his best moments, Brian lives out his deep desire to be a great dad, husband, boss, and friend. He responds to his wife and kids in a nurturing, kind, and patient manner, and he treats his friends and coworkers with respect.

But in his worst moments, Brian is not fun to be around. He can be insensitive, impatient, and demanding. He overreacts when certain people let him down. In those moments, he knows he causes damage to his most important relationships, eroding the tender bond that his typically good behavior creates. He sees how he is hurting others, and it bothers him deeply.

Brian often stops by my office after having one of his destructive outbursts. He wants to understand: "Why do I keep behaving this way?"

I also have an executive coaching client—we'll call her Gwen—who is a district manager for a global company. On good days, she relates to her husband, kids, friends, coworkers, and boss with kindness and courage. By nature, she is a helper and nurturer, and she strives to live out her natural wiring without losing her own voice. Her desire to be a gentle, strong adult is sincere.

But on too many days, Gwen finds she lacks backbone. She caves when her boss, a marketing vice president, makes excessive demands. She routinely picks up the slack when a peer underperforms. She tackles a long to-do list when her husband and children don't do their share of managing the home. Certain people always seem to get the best of her. In the heat of battle, she fails to advocate for what she believes is right, surrendering her voice and giving in to the demands of others at the cost of her own health and self-worth.

I met with Gwen in her office after one of these destructive moments of giving in and people pleasing. She was distraught. Gwen, like Brian, wants to understand: "Why do I keep behaving this way?"

Ever feel like Brian or Gwen? I do. I believe, in some way, independent of our gender, ethnicity, sexual orientation, or socioeconomic status, their story is our story.

Perhaps you have people in your life who regularly trigger you, either toward irritation and anger or toward submission and surrender. Perhaps you picked up this book because you want to learn how to change your reactions. You want insight or tools to help you improve your relationships. If so, we have a lot in common.

I can trace my interest in improving relationships back to a single moment many years ago. I was sitting at my desk in the loft of our home one balmy afternoon and reflecting on my life. From the outside, it looked as if I had it made. I was married to a lovely woman. I had a bunch of great kids. I loved my job as an emergency medicine physician in a trauma center. I served as an elder in my church.

And yet things were not as they appeared.

When I looked beneath the surface, I spotted relational tension everywhere I looked. Things were strained in my marriage. I felt a nagging distance from my kids. I wasn't managing conflict well at work or at church. And I was estranged from one of my parents.

*Why is all of this relational pain around me?*

The deeper I explored, the more I began to sense that other people weren't the problem, and that perhaps it was my automatic, unproductive reactions to people that were at the center of the problem. That's when a painful reality sunk in: the unifying thread running through all of my relational chaos was me. *Dang!*

On the one hand, the reality that much of the problem lies within me was disappointing. But, on the other hand, I felt empowered. I realized I couldn't change anyone else, but I could change myself. I was curious: *What is it about me that keeps landing me in these reactive moments? Why do I respond so poorly and with such consistency?*

About that same time, I was doing a lot of reading about the concept of story, not in the literary sense, but in the personal sense, as in "each of us has a story." What I discovered is that our story impacts our reality today. This truth prompted the title of this book. Our past is present today in every aspect of our lives, influencing our thoughts and behaviors and reactions. This is why attention to our story is so important. Story matters. My story matters. And so does yours.

I was a skeptic at first. But I've long since come to learn that exploring where I came from and how I got where I am today brings healing and growth, not just in my relationships, but in every area of my life. I am slowly doing the rest of my life better as a result.

This reality sparked what would become a lifelong ambition: understanding and improving my own behavior in relationships. That afternoon at my desk, I set a life goal: *From this moment forward, I want to screw up my relationships a little bit less every day.*

Not a very lofty goal, right? But I knew I hadn't developed my relational patterns overnight and changing those patterns would take time, practice, and more than a little hard work. Pursuing this goal led me to spend the past twenty-five years exploring healthy and unhealthy relationships; specifically, the origins of destructive relational patterns and how we can break free from them.

Now here I am, many years later. I have close relationships with my kids. I have deep friendships with people I value and admire. And my wife and I share the sweetest marriage I know. I certainly don't count myself a relationship expert, but I have become my own expert on how to screw up my relationships a little bit less every day.

In short, by improving how I relate, I am doing the rest of my life better and getting the life I want.

The concepts and principles I've learned on this journey have found their way into the consulting, coaching, and training I do. In fact, the topic of this book emerged from Relate, a series of workshops I developed and field-tested with thousands of participants in recent years. I have changed the names and identifying details of the individuals in the stories I share to protect their privacy. Any similarity to actual people or events is purely coincidental.

*Past Present* is laid out in three parts:

- Part I explores the concept of story: why it's so important to know your story and how to define and understand the concept of that story going forward.
- Part II examines some practical tools and strategies for understanding and telling your story. You'll discover two different vantage points from which to view your past, explore deeper nuances of your story, and learn about some bumps you'll want to avoid when sharing your story with others. You'll also see what it looks like when the painful parts of your story and your "lizard brain" collide.
- Part III explores the question, How do I heal my broken story? Once you've identified parts of your story that need healing, you'll learn how to process and heal those broken parts, resolve any unhelpful relational patterns that are getting in the way, and take steps toward better relationships a little more each day.

My hope is that reading this book will give you greater insights into yourself and your most important relationships.

However, I want you to do more than just read these pages. I hope you will act on them by taking simple steps to screw up your relationships a little less. I believe it will be as transformative for you as it has been for me.

Here's to doing the rest of our lives better!

# PART ONE

# WHY STORY MATTERS

Most self-help books send us in the direction of focusing on today or tomorrow, which admittedly makes sense. Don't we need to do some things differently moving forward in order to do the rest of our lives better? Yet few of us are able to sustain those well-intentioned changes we think will improve our lives. I believe this is because we don't understand the profoundly deep connection between our yesterdays and our tomorrows.

This is a book about stories—your story and mine. And like every good story, it's best to start at the beginning. In a good movie script, backstory matters. What happened to a beloved character before the current plot points explains so much. It gives us insight into that character's motivations and decisions. It makes the story meaningful and riveting.

The same is true in the story of our lives. Backstory matters. In part I of this book, we start at the beginning by asking two key questions: What is a story and why does understanding our story matter? In chapter 1, we explore why pausing to pay attention to our stories is not merely helpful but essential in helping us do our lives better. In chapter 2, we learn how to get clear on our stories, mining them for insights that empower us in our relationships.

Better relationships hold the key to doing life better. Let's dive in and build the crucial foundation of understanding your story.

# ONE

# Story: Why Bother?

God made humankind because God loves stories.

—Elie Wiesel, *The Gates of the Forest*

## NO CLUE

As the paramedics rushed the gurney into room 10, the looks on their faces told me this patient was in trouble. The young man lying before me was unconscious, his skin pale and covered with sweat.

This case began like so many others in the emergency department of Deaconess Medical Center, where I was working my favorite shift—the night shift—as an attending physician. The ambulance arrived with lights flashing and sirens blaring but no information on the patient: no history, no clues to his condition, nothing. He was simply "found down," meaning unconscious and unattended. Was this an assault? An overdose? A stroke?

An attempted suicide? A heart attack? Diabetic coma? Mental breakdown?

In those first two or three precious minutes of a patient's arrival, my role was twofold: to stabilize and to gather data.

This young John Doe was in serious trouble. He was comatose. His heart raced at more than 180 beats per minute and his blood pressure, which had been wildly fluctuating, was now dangerously low. No immediate physical findings gave clues to the cause of his condition. No needle tracks, breath odors, signs of trauma, pupillary changes, or visible injuries.

The ER staff and I began our quick first look at the patient. I intubated him to secure his airway, and the team began vital sign monitoring and blood draws.

I turned to the paramedic who had brought him in and asked, "What's his story?"

"His girlfriend found him down in the hallway outside his apartment," he said. "She has no clue what happened or how long he'd been down."

"Find anything inside his apartment?"

"Nothing unusual," he said. "No drug paraphernalia, no sign of violence."

No help.

Within the first few minutes, we ruled out the usual culprits behind a found-down John Doe, which included obvious trauma, opiate overdose, heart arrhythmia, low/high blood sugar, catastrophic central nervous system injury, or carbon monoxide poisoning. Yet this young man was deteriorating fast. His heart rate began fluctuating again and was now soaring at over two hundred beats per minute. When I glanced at his EKG, it showed signs of impending collapse.

"Blood pH, 6.9," a nurse said.

All terrible signs. And I was no closer to knowing what was killing him. If we didn't do something right now to reverse whatever was going on, he'd be dead in a matter of minutes.

About then, the charge nurse rushed into the trauma room. "His girlfriend just arrived," she said. "We took her to the family room."

I made a beeline to the private room reserved for the families of critically ill patients, and I hoped this woman could offer some clues as to what happened to her boyfriend. She sat alone, looking a little worried, but not nearly as worried as I knew she should be. I approached and introduced myself.

"Hi, I'm Scott Vaudrey, and I'm the doctor treating your boyfriend."

"Is he okay?" she asked. "What's wrong with him?"

"I was hoping you could tell me," I said. "Do you have any idea what happened?"

"No, I just found him passed out like that in the hallway."

"Does he have any medical problems that you know of?"

"No."

"Does he take any medication?"

"No."

"Does he have allergies to any drugs?"

"No."

"Does he use drugs or abuse any substances?"

"No."

"Has he ever tried to hurt himself or ever talked about wanting to hurt himself?"

"No."

This woman was not exactly brimming with information.

"Okay, well, thank you for answering my questions," I said. "We'll keep you informed."

I turned to hurry back to the trauma room, but before I reached the door, I stopped to ask one more question. "Is there *anything* about your boyfriend—anything at all—that you think might be useful for me to know?"

She took her time pondering my question. With my patient at death's door, every second mattered.

"Well," she said, "there is one thing . . ."

"Yes?"

"He works with a lot of weird chemicals at his job."

"Seriously? Like, what kind of weird chemicals?"

"Like . . . cyanide," she replied matter-of-factly.

I turned and sprinted toward the young man's room. Halfway there, an overhead page sounded: "Dr. Vaudrey, phone call, line 2."

Back in the ER, I picked up the phone. On the other end was one of my favorite police sergeants, a guy I'd come to know well over my years on the job. He had responded to the call on this young man and was still at the apartment clearing the scene.

"Scott, you'll never believe what I just found in this kid's bathroom," he said.

And in unison we both said, "Cyanide!"

Here's the thing about cyanide toxicity. Every board-certified ER doc in the country knows how to treat it, not because it's common (it's not), but because a scenario involving cyanide poisoning is always on our national board exams.[1]

Cyanide ingestion is exceedingly rare. Accidental cyanide toxicity can occur when someone inhales the smoke from a house or industrial fire. But intentional cyanide ingestion is almost unheard of, mainly because cyanide isn't readily accessible to the general public. Most ER docs will go their entire careers without ever treating an acute cyanide ingestion.

Not all poisons have an antidote, but luckily for this young man, cyanide poisoning does. The treatment includes administering a series of specific drugs in a specific dosing sequence. Every hospital pharmacy stocks these drugs in a user-friendly package nicknamed the "Lilly cyanide kit" (for Eli Lilly, the pharmaceutical company that created it). We secured the Lilly kit, rushed it to room 10, and began administering the drugs.

Within a couple of minutes, this young man's symptoms began making a dramatic reversal. Soon he was sitting up in bed and eating Jell-O. He went from death's door to Jell-O in a matter of minutes. It was remarkable to witness.

I was a well-trained emergency physician, working alongside an amazing team of nurses and staff in an ER with an excellent reputation. I had many years of experience diagnosing found-down patients. But even if I'd had instant access to the best consultants in the world or all the latest research articles about found-down comatose patients to help manage this patient's presenting symptoms, none of it would have helped. He would have been dead before I found the answer. Why? Because the answer wasn't in his symptoms but in his story.

## WHY YOUR STORY MATTERS

I think of this case every time I talk to someone about why it's so important to examine and share our stories, especially when we're trying to break free of self-defeating behaviors and improve our relationships. It vividly illustrates what can go wrong when we try to fix personal and relational problems by focusing on symptoms alone. Symptoms are simply the outward behaviors that cause relational problems. (For Brian and Gwen from the introduction, the symptoms were impatience and people pleasing, respectively.)

When we go after symptoms, we can read all the latest books and seek wisdom from the best mentors or therapists and still remain stuck. That's because the critical clue we need isn't in our symptoms. It's in our stories. Reading books and consulting mentors or therapists are excellent ideas, and I believe *everyone* should read lots of books and go to counseling. But these efforts need to take place in *addition to*, not *instead of*, understanding and sharing our stories.

I have known many people who have been in counseling for years, but because they chose not to deal with their past in those counseling sessions, little has changed in their relational worlds. They are still stuck in self-defeating behaviors and still struggling with the same relationship-damaging patterns. They periodically change therapists because the last one "couldn't help me." But they continue in the same cycle of relational pain because they are determined to focus on their symptoms rather than deal with their root issues.

Based on the research of many experts, my personal experience in dealing with my own relational junk, and years of walking alongside thousands of people during their relational crises, I have come to believe that we cannot make sustained progress in resolving our unproductive relational patterns without having some clarity about how we came to possess those patterns in the first place.

Most of us learned these patterns when we were young. Back then, our behavioral and relational patterns shielded or protected us. For Brian, his impatience and angry outbursts kept bullies (particularly his older brother) at bay. For Gwen, her compliance and withholding her protests allowed her to coexist with her critical mother and volatile father. These defense mechanisms were a means to an end. They were Band-Aids covering the real problems beneath the surface. Getting clear on how and why we do what we do is essential if we want to grow beyond the patterns of yesterday that are causing us trouble today.

To say it another way: *We can't get where we want to go until we're clear on where we've been.*

I believe, to my core, that your story is your pathway to healing. If you are willing to engage your past and your story with courage, I believe you will discover the clues to help you get unstuck and do the rest of your life better.

## TWO FORMS OF RESISTANCE

When I suggest that digging into family-of-origin issues is a necessary step for understanding relational patterns, I often encounter two forms of resistance. And I get it. In fact, I put up the same forms of resistance many years ago when I was first asked to tell my story.

The first form of resistance sounds like this: "I don't want to be one of those whiners who blames Mommy for all my problems. My parents were good people. They did the best they could. In fact, I had it better than most. I certainly had it better than my parents did."

If you're in this camp, breathe easy. I agree with you completely. This outlook is a good and healthy place to be. There is nothing about where we're headed in the coming chapters that seeks to pin the blame on anyone else for our problems. In fact, one of the benefits I discovered when I began to understand my story was that I was actually better equipped to take ownership of the patterns that were holding me back. Even if some of my choices and behaviors were heavily influenced by my family of origin, I am now the only one responsible for those behaviors and choices. The same is true of you. Looking back at your family of origin isn't about looking for someone to blame. It's about gaining insight and understanding. You're seeking to answer the question "Why do I do what I do?" so you can choose differently in the future.

The second form of resistance sounds like this: "The past is dead and gone. I can't change my past, so why revisit it? No sense in crying over spilled milk. Forget the past. I just want to look to the future."

I'm sympathetic to this line of thinking as well. For too many years, this was my go-to argument when friends or mentors suggested I needed to do some story work. But there is one problem with this line of thinking: it's not true. As American author William Faulkner wrote, "The past is never dead. It's not even past."[2]

If you just want to look to the future, here's my invitation: humor me on this exploration of your past despite your reluctance and see what good can come from it. I was well into my thirties before I overcame my resistance to examining my story. I regret I did not engage this healing, liberating work sooner. I've found that those of us who use this form of resistance often have the most to gain by engaging our story. When we honestly face the reality that patterns from our past are contributing to the relational disharmony in our present, pathways to lasting healing will open up. The investment of time and energy is well worth it.

The past is not past. The past is present.

It takes courage to dive into our stories and get to the root of why we do what we do. And once we realize that we all have relational work to do, we will find the courage we need to answer the questions "How is it that I have come to this place?" and "Why do I keep behaving in a way I know isn't working?" Addressing these questions is an essential step to living a life of maximal impact and relational fulfillment. We all want to do the rest of our lives better. And the first step is to get curious about our stories. Let's begin by defining what story is in the next chapter.

## For Reflection

Spend some time reflecting on the questions below by journaling your responses. Then, if you are comfortable, share your observations with someone who is safe and trustworthy (a close friend, a therapist, or a significant other).

- How open and motivated are you to explore your past?
- If you have some resistance to examining your family of origin and story, what do you think you

are afraid of? For example, are you afraid of being perceived as a whiner? Wasting time? Reliving the abuse? Challenging a "perfect" childhood?

## T W O

# What Is Story?

You are your stories. No one's story exists alone.
They have shaped how you see yourself, the world,
and your place in it.

—Daniel Taylor, *Tell Me a Story*

To know our plot is the first step in changing it.

—Dan Allender, *To Be Told*

You're on a journey toward some target or preferred future. Inevitably, though, whether from situations beyond your control or from poor choices, you get a little (or a lot) off course. The first step toward getting back on track is to assess where you are today:

13

Much of the exploration we'll do together in the coming chapters is designed to help you better understand your current coordinates. Where are you? How did you get here? This is important data if you hope to write a new plot and chart the rest of your life toward that preferred future. So you must start at understanding "here" (the starting point from which you'll do the rest of your life).

Coordinates matter, especially when we are prone to getting off course. This is as true in life as it is in mapping a road trip.

To illustrate the importance of knowing our coordinates, allow me to confess an embarrassing truth: when I get behind the wheel of a car, I tend to get lost. Actually, I tend to get distracted, and then I get lost. I start listening to an audiobook or thinking about my day, and before I know it, I have no idea where I am. Even though I was an early adopter of GPS, it hasn't helped much. My smartphone map isn't smart enough to hold my attention while I'm driving, and I've become immune to the semi-polite mockery of my old-school GPS narrator and her repeated "Recalculating."

For nearly twenty years I lived in the suburbs of Chicago, about an hour south of the Wisconsin border. On more than one occasion, when I thought I was driving home, I'd suddenly see an upcoming road sign, Welcome to Wisconsin. On one such occasion, I was driving a forty-foot motor home that got about six miles to the gallon—an expensive mistake!

Now, imagine you are the unfortunate one trying to help me navigate. Maybe you invited me to your house for dinner. You're a good cook. I'm a good eater. It's a great plan! I accept your invitation, get your address, and type it into Google Maps on my phone. What could possibly go wrong?

I get in my car on the agreed-upon night and begin driving. But sure enough, I soon realize I am lost. I call and say, "I have a little problem. I'm trying to get to your house but I'm lost. Can you help me?"

What's the first question that comes out of your mouth?

"Where are you?"

Of course! You first ask me where I am, because it would be foolish to immediately tell me to turn left or turn around without first knowing where I am. You can't give me useful directions until you know my starting place, my coordinates. So you start by asking, "Where are you?"

To which I reply, "I have no idea" (my typical answer).

Now what? How are you going to help me get to my desired destination?

Most of the time, in this scenario, the person giving me directions responds, "Okay, look around. Give me some land-marks. What do you see?"

Great idea! I look around. "Well," I respond, "I'm at an inter-section, and on one corner I see a McDonald's, on another corner I see a Starbucks, and across the street I see a Target."

I've just described almost every intersection in suburban North America. Not helpful.

Even worse, I sometimes misunderstand where I actually am. There have been times when I told the other person where I *thought* I was, but I was wrong. Other times, I've been lost and unaware.

On the day I drove our motor home into Wisconsin, if my wife had called me when I was a mile from the border and asked, "Where are you?" I would have said, "I'm almost home!" While I believed this to be true, I was grossly mistaken because I didn't know I was lost.

If we inaccurately describe our current circumstances in life—whether intentionally or unintentionally—we only lead others astray in their efforts to guide us to our preferred future. This is part of why so many of us can go to a counselor for years and yet stay stuck.

Back to dinner at your house. You asked, "Where are you?" and I was of no help. You asked for landmarks, and my answer didn't help you pinpoint where I was. Now what?

When our kids were teens and new drivers, we often found ourselves in this situation. New drivers tend to get lost, and most of our five kids learned to drive in the pre-GPS era. As a result, early in their driving careers, each needed to call home for directions after finding themselves lost. (Up to that point, the only person who regularly called home for directions was me.)

Here's how a typical conversation with one of our teens would go.

*Ring.*

**Me:** Hello.
**Teen:** Oh, um . . . Hi, Dad. Um . . . Is Mom home?
    [Our kids all knew I would be utterly useless in this situation.]
**Me:** Sure, I'll get her.

From this point on, I'd hear only my wife September's side of the conversation. She'd listen for a while, then I'd hear her ask the question.

**September:** Okay, honey, where are you?

Typically, the child had no idea where they were, and by the time they'd called to ask for help, they were a bit flustered. My wife has plenty of experience helping lost, flustered drivers because she is married to me. She would always masterfully complete two crucial tasks. First, she'd calmly reassure the driver she would stay with them and guide them as long as needed until they were back on track to their destination. Second, she'd ask the driver to retrace their steps.

> **September:** Okay, you just left for the mall a few minutes ago. Walk me through each turn you took after you left the house.

After listening, September would usually ask a clarifying question.

> **September:** So you turned right, onto Ela Road, went left on Algonquin, and then you turned *left* at Roselle? Hmm . . . I wonder if that's where you got off course. To get to the mall, you'd need to have turned right at Roselle, then left on Golf.

Then hearing the details of their journey, September could usually piece together the answer to the where-are-you question. Then she'd give the lost child a sense of where they were and offer some next steps to get them back on track to their destination.

You can probably see where I'm headed with this, right? September helped our kids identify their coordinates by asking them to retrace their steps. In essence, she asked them to tell their story. The same thing needs to happen with you and me when we're lost in the tangle of self-defeating behaviors. *Our story is the answer to the question "Where are you?"*

When we find ourselves in an uncomfortable place relationally, we know we are lost, but we often don't know how we got lost. When we seek the help of a friend, counselor, pastor, or mentor, and they ask us to describe our situation, they are essentially asking, "Where are you?"

Then we look around and describe our current surroundings or experiences. But when it comes to relational difficulties, we don't know the answer to the where-are-you question. What's worse, when we try to explain our coordinates, we often give incomplete or unhelpful information:

- "My marriage is hurting."
- "My kids are out of control."
- "I can't stop eating/drinking/using."
- "I lost my temper with my spouse—again."
- "I always end up hating my job."
- "I can't say no."

While these pieces of information might be accurate, they don't really offer much insight into the deeper question, "How did you come to this place?" They're the equivalent of a lost driver saying, "I'm near a McDonald's and a Starbucks," which is not helpful when it comes to understanding how you got there. At this point, you need insights that can only come from retracing your steps.

There are limitless pathways that lead to distressed marriages, destructive behaviors, and strained relationships. As a result, there are limitless steps we can take to get to a better place, namely, a preferred future. But for a step to be helpful, it must be tailored to the path we took to get here. The most helpful, productive step must be based on context and history. If our friends, counselors, or mentors don't have clarity on where we've been, their only resort would be to offer generic directions ("Turn right") before they know our coordinates. Generic directions are unlikely to help the situation and can actually make things worse.

Here are some examples of generic directions:

- "Go to an anger-management class."
- "Put porn-accountability software on your computer."
- "Use 'I' statements when you argue with your spouse."
- "Read your Bible."
- "Stop hanging out with unhealthy people."
- "Pray and meditate."
- "Stop going to bars after work."

These are all good and wise steps. There is nothing wrong with them. I've offered these very suggestions many times. However, *by themselves* they won't get at the root issues. They fail to answer the question "How is it that you got to this place?" Therefore, the benefits of such suggestions are limited. They won't bring about lasting change. If we want to make changes in our lives that stick, we must go after root issues.

We can do the rest of our relational lives better. But to do so, we must first understand how we got to this place in the relationship. We must ask ourselves, "Where am I?" and "How did I get here?" We need to know the roots of our own stories.

# A FOUNDATIONAL
# UNDERSTANDING OF STORY

To capture the essence of what I mean when I use the term *story*, I want to share some foundational insights from two authors who have written extensively on the topic.[1] Daniel Taylor is an English professor, and Dan Allender is a psychologist and theologian. They have PhDs in very different academic disciplines, and yet both have arrived at similar views on the meaning and purpose of story.

These brief quotes from their writings will inform our understanding of story for the rest of this book:

> You are your stories. No one's story exists alone. They have shaped how you see yourself, the world, and your place in it. If your present life story is broken or diseased, it can be made well. Or, if necessary, it can be replaced by a story that has a plot worth living. . . . If I now know, or think I know, that some of those stories were distortions, or unfair, or covered up evil, that is only because I kept listening, discovering other stories that should have been told me before. The best antidote to incomplete or faulty stories is more stories from different tellers. (Taylor, *Tell Me a Story*, 1, 13)

> I can't change my tragedies, nor can I really eliminate (fully) the characters in my story, but I can write a new plot. To do so requires reengaging the tragedies of my life with new patterns. . . . To know our plot is the first step in changing it. (Allender, *To Be Told*, 19)

What do you notice when you read these descriptions of what story is? Do you recognize the similarities? Both scholars suggest you and I *are* our stories. We are constituted and formed by our past experiences. In addition, both experts recognize that some parts of our stories are marred and less than perfect. And yet there is also the good news: if your "life story is broken or diseased, it can be made well."

Therapists often describe the process of rewriting our stories as narrative repair. Louis Cozolino, an expert on neuroscience and human relationships, noted, "Therapists hope to teach their clients that not only can they edit their present story, but they can also be authors of new stories."[2] Stories can be healed. As a result, we can do our relationships and the rest of our lives better.

I find this reassuring. The broken parts of my story can be repaired, healed, or, if necessary, an entire plot can be replaced. The implications of this truth are profound: we are *influenced* by our past, but we are not *determined* by it.

Allender's statement, "To know our plot is the first step in changing it," validates the principle that we can't get to where we want to go until we are clear on where we have been.

Taylor states our stories shape how we see ourselves, the world, and our place in it. I would add, for people of faith, stories also shape how we see God and how we think God sees us.

I have found hope and freedom in the prospect of repairing the broken parts of my story with a new plot. I have also seen many people experience emotional freedom and relational success because they engaged their stories and did the work to make them well. They wrote a new plot for themselves.

Where do we begin to write a new plot? How do we heal

our stories? We begin with two critical early steps: we attack our problems at the root, and then we tell new stories.

## ATTACK PROBLEMS AT THE ROOT

For most of us, the primary motivation to explore our story and write a new plot is to find relief from discomfort or disappointment. What is it for you?

Perhaps you are depressed or anxious. You think you may be a people pleaser, or you worry that you drink too much. Perhaps you're defensive, resentful, angry, or lonely. Whatever the reason, you're reading this book because you want your life to look different in some way, large or small, and you're committed to understanding these troubling patterns of thought or behavior so you can improve them.

If you're like me, once you become convinced you need to change or grow in some way, you want to get busy trying to correct that issue. It's good and necessary to make such concerted effort because your self-defeating behaviors hurt your relationships. You may buy a book on the issue that is plaguing you. You might see a therapist about the problem or begin attending a recovery program. All of these are great ideas. But merely attacking the problem of the outward behavior alone won't be sufficient. You need more than willpower. You need more than behavior modification. Until you address the behavior at its origin—its roots—you will not find lasting relief.

An analogy may help here. If you've ever had a home with a lawn, then you've likely had the dismaying experience of discovering thousands of dandelions suddenly blooming across your yard. You know if you don't do something soon, those dandelions will spread, and the problem will only get worse.

Imagine taking a pair of scissors and showing those weeds who's boss. You cut the yellow heads off all those nasty weeds and toss the vanquished intruders into the trash. You walk across your yard and take in the peaceful view of a beautiful lawn. No yellow dandelions. Things look fantastic—today. But soon more yellow dandelions appear. Until you dig out each dandelion by its root, the weeds will continue to plague your yard.

Attacking our problem behaviors at the level of the behaviors themselves is a lot like cutting off dandelion heads. It might look and feel nice for a while, but it won't be long until the problematic behaviors return.

Imagine you turn to someone in your family for help because you sense you might be developing a drinking problem, and their response is to say, "Stop drinking!" Or imagine you seek help for your strained marriage, and your therapist says, "Use 'I' statements when you argue," "Stop nagging," or "Go on date nights." These ideas might help in the moment—you look around and see no more weeds—but the problematic roots remain. If you use quick-fix strategies, the weeds *always* come back, often more abundantly than before.

Of course, we all know the only way to get rid of literal weeds is by attacking them at the root. This is also true of relational weeds, which are the consequences of our unhelpful patterns of behavior. Our stories reveal the roots of those behaviors, which is why we can't get to where we want to go until we're clear on where we've been.

One of the negative patterns (weeds) in my life relates to my futile attempts to protect myself by controlling others. When I eventually came to recognize this was a problem in my marriage, I knew I had to take responsibility. I wanted to stop being so controlling. So I began telling myself, "Stop being controlling!" My strategy to tackle this destructive relational pattern was to employ behavior modification: I'd simply try to quit controlling September. I mustered all my willpower and tried *really hard* to change. It didn't work.

My desire to stop being so controlling was reasonable. My wife was grateful for my efforts. And the strategy I'd need to deploy included trying really hard to stop; no change worth making comes without some effort. But there needed to be more to my strategy. With effort alone, I made some initial progress through sheer determination and force of will. But time and time again, I drifted back to my controlling ways and the pattern of behavior I wanted to leave behind. Because I hadn't gotten to the root of the issue, I consistently relapsed. And with each relapse, I felt discouraged, struggled with self-doubt, and lost hope. Worse, I broke a deeper level of trust with my wife. Snipping off my dandelion heads was costly.

But here's the good news. Once I began examining my story, I noticed some distorted beliefs I'd picked up when I was young; distortions in how I saw myself, the world, and my place in it. I was able to see how those distortions were at the root of my unproductive pattern of controlling behavior. I had never been consciously aware of those beliefs. I'd never articulated them. Yet I now saw how they animated my behavior in *all* of my relationships.

As soon as I became aware of how these distorted beliefs were driving my unhelpful behaviors, I was better able to address my control issue at both the weed and the root levels. I was able to address the *whole* dandelion, both above and below ground, and today I experience (mostly) sustained success in this area. My wife tells me I'm no longer a controlling jerk in my marriage. And if I do slip back into my old controlling ways, I can usually spot it and make a quick course correction.

Choosing a strategy of examining my story to better understand my behavior—rather than just a strategy of willpower and behavior modification—has made all the difference. Going after the roots rather than (or in addition to) snipping off the dandelion heads is actually less work and far more effective in the long run. It's a strategy that lasts.

## TELL NEW STORIES BY LISTENING TO OTHERS' STORIES

In addition to attacking our problems at the root, we heal our past narratives by telling new stories. Successful narrative repair requires telling newer, truer stories about ourselves. Interestingly, one of the most effective pathways to learning how to create a new story of our own requires that we listen to the stories of others.

No one, no matter how idyllic their past may be, has a story free from distortions. It's part of the human experience. We are all broken, and we are all beautiful. When we hear the stories of other people, we gain insight into our own stories. Only when we hear the stories of others can we experience new realities and possibilities for ourselves and our futures. Daniel Taylor observed, "The best antidote to incomplete or faulty stories is more stories from different tellers."[3]

This statement is a bit counterintuitive, and I didn't really believe this the first time I read it. But I have since learned there is something profoundly healing and redemptive in simply telling *and listening* to each other's stories. I am regularly blown away when I witness the power of sharing and hearing stories. It's a primary pathway to healing for the people in the relational workshops I teach and the coaching work I do, and it has figured prominently in my own healing and growth.

When I was growing up, I believed my childhood was normal and average. Most children believe this to be true about their stories, because they have little else to compare them to. However, after hearing the stories of many others, I learned that my story—and, in fact, *everyone's story*—is far from average. Every story is wildly unique. My story, like yours, has moments of profound exhilaration, delight, and joy, as well as moments of heartache and tragedy.

As a result of hearing other people's stories, I've seen how parts of my own story are beautiful and exceptional. This reality has left me even more grateful to my parents and some of my past teachers for the unique opportunities and formative experiences they provided. Similarly, as a result of listening to the stories of others, I can see the gaps or problematic parts of my own story. I've recognized that, like everyone else, there are painful parts of my story that need a new plot. This concept is vitally important for us to grasp, not to blame our parents, families, schools, and so on but to make sense of where we find ourselves today. We gather data—the good parts and the broken parts—to both celebrate the good and repair the broken parts of our stories, the roots, that subconsciously contribute to our pain today.

When we witness how others experience our story, we are able to see the details of our narrative in a new way, through a new lens. Watching someone else respond emotionally to our story offers us the gift of an outside perspective. The reactions and observations of others often help us recalibrate our experience, inviting us to either celebrate or grieve the parts of our story we thought were insignificant. Often, by sharing our stories and listening to the stories of others, we find tremendous relief in the realization that we are not alone, affirming that our highs and lows are more normal than we thought.

## A Med School Lesson in Telling and Hearing Stories

This reminds me of my first year of medical school. There was a point when I felt overwhelmed by a particular subject. In the solitary moments of studying early one morning, I entertained the following belief: *Maybe the med school's admissions committee overestimated me. Maybe I don't have what it takes. Maybe I'm not cut out for medicine.* I harbored that worry for several days. Then, during a late-night study session with a friend, he confessed that he was struggling with a particular class and starting to worry that maybe his selection into med school was an error by the admissions committee. He worried that, as a medical student, he was a fraud. I was shocked! I knew my friend to be incredibly smart and competent. I shared with him that I was laboring under the same fears. He, too, was shocked.

This conversation was a pivotal moment for me. Through my friend's vulnerability in sharing his story, I found the courage to share mine. Then we were both able to rightsize our fears and find confidence and reassurance.

I experienced the redemptive power of storytelling that day. My friend and I ultimately ended up doing well in medical school and getting our first choices for residency. However, had it not been for his honesty in the early weeks of our first year, we may have labored on for who knows how long with the erroneous, stress-inducing distortions that we were not good enough. The intersection of our stories proved healing, refuted our distorted beliefs, and infused reality and confidence into our lives.

The healing that took place over the seemingly small fear that *maybe I'm not cut out for medicine* actually went much deeper for me. It struck at an even more destructive belief. Up to that point, whenever I was faced with a relationship or situation that risked exposing me to failure or embarrassment, I would find a way to bail. *Better to ditch the relationship or opportunity than to risk embarrassment* was the lie I told myself. This created an unhealthy transiency and lack of commitment in my relationships.

The narrative repair that came from sharing, examining, and recalibrating my belief by sharing my story that day taught me to be quicker to do so in the future. And as I practiced sharing my story in other aspects of my life—and listening to the stories of others—it started a cascade of exposing and healing more significant and potentially destructive distorted beliefs.

I saw how others survived embarrassment or failure and realized I could too. I saw how others reaped the fruit of taking risks, and it gave me confidence to be a greater risk taker. Taking risks and seeking opportunities for sharing my story was worth it. And lasting relationships were worth it too.

It's reassuring to know we can change the unwanted emotional and relational patterns that trouble us by attacking an issue both at the behavioral level and at its root. We can change the trajectory of the troublesome parts of our emotional and relational world and write new plots for a better tomorrow.

# For Reflection

Spend some time reflecting on the questions below by journaling your responses. Then, if you are comfortable, share your observations with someone who is safe and trustworthy (a close friend, a therapist, or a significant other).

- What story lines from your past might be affecting your relationships today?
- What broken part of your story would you most like to rewrite or make well?
- How well do you think you are doing in sharing your story with others? Assess yourself on a scale of 1 (I never share) to 10 (I share at appropriate levels freely and openly). If your score is a seven or below, what could you do this week to start sharing your story more freely?

# PART TWO

# UNDERSTANDING
# YOUR STORY

In part I, we learned that by examining and telling our stories we can address our unproductive behavioral patterns. But what does it look like to write a new plot? If you're like me, you find the prospect of writing a new plot both exciting and daunting. That's normal. I'm often asked, "How do I *know* my story so I can write a new plot?" This is the question we'll tackle next.

The process of truly understanding our own stories is the most critical and most difficult step when it comes to maximizing the best parts of our past and healing the broken parts. When people fail in their efforts to heal the broken parts of their story, it's not because it was too hard but because they didn't pay close enough attention to really knowing and understanding their plot in the first place.

In part II, we tackle the task of understanding our story plots by looking at them from two vantage points: the *who* of our stories (Who are the primary actors?) and the *what* of our stories (What are the action points?). Through these exercises, we'll gain insight into why we see ourselves, the world, and our place in it the way we do, and thus, what's behind the ways we involuntarily sabotage our relationships.

# THREE

# Characters: Understanding the *Who* of Your Story

Often, a large portion of a client's story has been unconsciously imposed by past generations of their families. What makes it especially hard to edit is that much of this origin is unconscious.

—Louis Cozolino, *Why Therapy Works*

One of my favorite things to do while traveling is to explore new cities and neighborhoods on foot. So before I take a trip, I open Google Maps and pull up a map of the area on my laptop. I first zoom out to get a bird's-eye view of the state or region where I'm headed, so I can understand where this city lies in relationship to the rest of the state. Then I zoom in to see the city itself, so I can get an overview of the regions within. Finally, I zoom in closer, to within a mile or two of where I'll be staying, so I can see what's within walking distance. Only then can I know which direction I should start walking after I arrive. Exploring my new surroundings without first knowing the lay of the land would be much less fruitful—and much slower. So I start with a map.

A similar principle applies when it comes to exploring the characters in our stories. Taking the time to get a lay of the land first—zooming out, then zooming in closer and closer—will make our explorations more likely to be fruitful and effective. And one of the most helpful maps for capturing a wider view of our stories before zooming in is a tool called the genogram.

## WHAT IS A GENOGRAM?

A genogram is a map of the characters in your story. It's a visual depiction of the people in your family and, more important, the cultures, events, and characteristics of those people over the last several generations. Essentially, a genogram is an intentional and contemporary genealogy or family tree that provides a useful lens through which to get the lay of the land in your story.

Genograms have been around for centuries, and people draw genograms for a variety of reasons. Historians use them to trace the genealogy of important figures when writing a biography. Doctors rely on genograms to track and predict inherited diseases. In fact, mapping one's family in the context of story came into popular clinical usage for physicians after the 1986 release of *Genograms in Family Assessment* by Monica McGoldrick and Randy Gerson.[1]

For our purposes, genograms help us identify and name generational patterns, traits, and environments that likely affected us as kids, both positively and negatively. Drawing your genogram enhances your understanding of the culture within which you were formed so you can better explore your story.

A significant benefit of drawing your genogram is that it gives you holistic insight into how you got to where you are today. It's the zoomed-out big-picture map of your life. Your genogram also becomes a useful tool to help you share your story with others.

I experienced this a number of years ago when one of the staff teams I led had a remarkable team-building day together. The ten of us met in a conference room lined with whiteboards. We spent the first hour drawing out our genograms individually, and then we spent the rest of the day gathered around each person's whiteboard. One at a time, we shared the highs and lows of our genogram and the insights we gained from the process. It bonded our team in significant ways, and we grew as individuals from what we shared with one another.

## DRAWING YOUR GENOGRAM

Now it's time to draw your own genogram, which we'll do in stages throughout the remainder of this chapter. First, we'll take a look at the basic structure of a genogram, and I'll give you some tips on how to get started. Then we'll zoom in and add some descriptors, which provide additional details. I'll walk you through how to add those to your genogram as well.[2] If you're one of those people who's tempted to read through this section but bypass the actual work of crafting your map, I strongly encourage you to resist that temptation! Do the work. I promise you'll be glad you did.

### The Basic Structure

The basic structure of a genogram includes shapes, lines, marks, and dates.

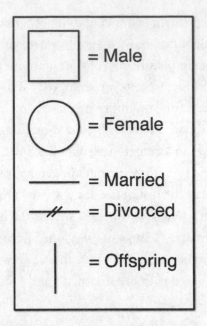

= Male

= Female

= Married

= Divorced

= Offspring

## Shapes and Lines

In all genograms, the people in your family are represented by two basic shapes: squares for males and circles for females.

Those shapes are connected by lines that indicate the kind of relationship, such as married, divorced, or offspring. In more complex genograms, there are several types of lines (jagged, broken, double, triple, etc.) that represent the nature of the relationship (committed, casual, temporary, etc.) or the emotional quality of the relationship (hostile, loving, distant, etc.). For our purposes, we'll primarily use solid lines.

Married couples are depicted by a horizontal line connecting the corresponding shapes.

Couples who cohabitate and have children together but are not married can be depicted with a dashed line. Couples who neither cohabitate nor marry but have children can be depicted by a squiggly line.

The convention is for the male to be drawn on the left of the horizontal line and the female on the right. But because of the great variety and transience of marital relationships (same-sex marriages, serial marriages, divorces, etc.), this is not always easy to do. As you add the shapes representing the people in your family, don't worry about strictly following this convention. Do what makes the most sense to you.

Offspring are noted by vertical lines that descend from the horizontal line that connects their parents. Offspring are listed in birth order from left to right (oldest to youngest).

There are two ways you can document siblings on your genogram. The most straightforward is to draw a descending vertical line for each offspring directly from the horizontal line that connects the parents.

However, this method gets tricky and difficult to draw when there are more than two children. A cleaner way is to have just one vertical line descend from the horizontal parent line to create a new bracket from which all the couple's offspring descend.

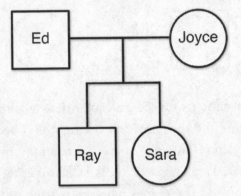

In this example, we're creating a genogram of Ray's family. His parents, Ed and Joyce, are married and have two children. Ray is represented by the square on the left. Ray's younger sister, Sara, is indicated by the circle to the right of Ray.

If Ray were to get married, we would expand the diagram.

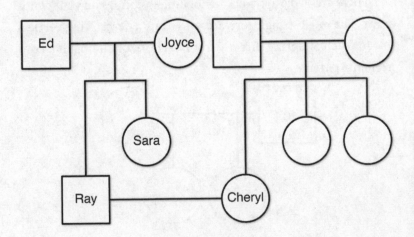

Ray married Cheryl, who is the oldest of three girls. Notice I lengthened the descending vertical lines of the people I want to follow—in this case, Ray and Cheryl. This makes it possible to draw a straight line between them.

By lengthening the lines on your genogram this way, it's much easier to draw the marriages and relationships you want to track.

## Marks and Dates

Genograms use a number of helpful marks to clarify relationships and events in someone's family story. We'll start by using two such marks to indicate when someone is deceased or divorced.

- *Deceased:* A large X over a shape indicates this person is deceased.
- *Divorced:* A double slash (\\) on a horizontal marriage line indicates the couple is divorced.

In the example on top of next page, the double slash between Ed and Joyce indicates that Ray's parents divorced and his mother remarried a man named Dave. This new marriage produced three more children. In addition, we can see from the large Xs that Ray's father and Cheryl's mother have passed away.

These additions to the family tree require us to widen the genogram. In order to capture the new marriage between Joyce and Dave, we break the convention of males always being on the left. This is fine for our purposes. Keeping the genogram easy to read is more important than convention.

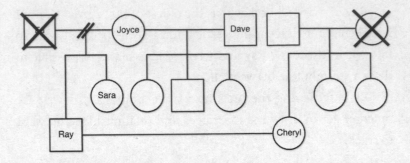

This genogram, which shows only two generations of one family, demonstrates how quickly a genogram can get messy when people marry, divorce, and remarry several times (common in many families). It can be difficult to keep the horizontal marriage lines horizontal. If someone in your family has been married several times, one option is to draw the lines going out from that person to their other spouses as spokes from the hub of a wheel.

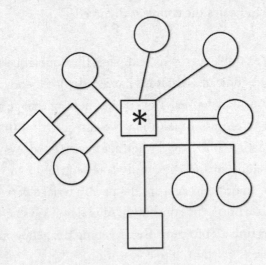

Do the best you can to capture your family relationships on your genogram, but feel free to focus mainly on the marriage(s) that affected you most as a child.

Similarly, the more generations and individuals you add to your genogram, the more complicated things become. Adding identifying details such as dates for births, deaths, marriages, and divorces can help you keep things straight.

- *Birth and death:* Dates written above a shape denote the dates of birth and death. Use the letter *b* to indicate date of birth ("b. 10/21/84" or simply "b. 1984"). Use the letter *d* to indicate the date of death (d. 1978).
- *Marriage and divorce:* Dates written above the horizontal lines connecting married couples denote the year of marriage and, if applicable, divorce. Use the letter *m* to indicate when the couple was married (m. 1947). If divorced, add a comma after the marriage date and then a *d* and the year of the divorce (m. 1947, d. 1961).

Here is what adding dates looks like on Ray's genogram:

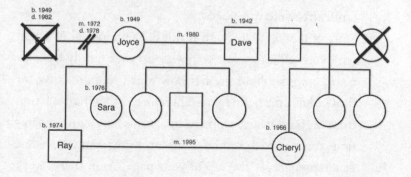

Now that we've covered the basics, let's begin sketching the foundational structure of your genogram. Here are some tips to get you started:

- *Gather materials:* Use a large sheet of blank paper, a whiteboard, or a flip chart. If drawing on paper, use a pencil with an eraser rather than a pen, since you'll likely need to make some adjustments as you go. If using a flip chart or whiteboard, take a photo of your genogram when it's complete so you can have a record of it for later use. Another strategy is to use sticky notes when initially trying to figure out how your family members might fit on the page.

- *Go deep:* If possible, go back at least two generations (your grandparents' generation). Go back to your great-grandparents if you feel those details might provide additional insight into your story.

- *Keep it simple by focusing on your formative years:* If you were adopted, grew up in a foster home, or were raised by people who weren't your parents, draw the family or families in which you spent your most formative years. If you grew up in more than one home, feel free to draw more than one genogram rather than trying to force a complicated family tree onto one page.

- *Start at the top:* Although it might seem logical to begin with yourself and work your way up your family tree, it's nearly impossible to predict how much room to leave for those who came before you. Therefore, rather than starting from the bottom and working up, decide how many generations you plan to draw and then start by mapping the oldest generation across the top of your page. From there, work your way down. In my genogram—which included my parents, grandparents, and great-grandparents—I needed to leave a considerable amount of space between my parents' shapes to accommodate all my aunts and uncles. Starting at the top kept me from running out of room and having to erase and start over.

- *Omit distant relatives:* It's not necessary to include distant relatives you didn't really know or who didn't play an influential role in your parents' or grandparents' lives. For example, I elected not to include the siblings of my great-grandparents or grandparents.

Draw out the basic structure of your genogram. Try to document at least two generations above you (parents and grandparents), and then we'll move on and add some descriptors.

## Descriptors

The shapes, lines, marks, and dates you've captured are the foundation of your genogram. Think of these elements as the black-and-white facts of your story. However, while they document information about your family, they don't tell the heart of your story, the living-color version. To understand the various factors and the people who helped shape the person you are today, it's necessary to add some critical elements to your genogram: descriptors.

Descriptors are the traits, events, and characteristics of the people, relationships, and family units that define the culture in which you grew up. Depending on how many generations you included in your genogram, there may be some individuals about whom you know little. You might need to contact relatives or friends to fill in the gaps in your knowledge.

When I was first working on my genogram, I realized I had big gaps in my knowledge about my mother's side of the family. So I called my mom and asked her to tell me stories of her family from her perspective. We shared several long conversations, during which I learned a ton of detailed, helpful information about the people who formed the woman who raised me. An added benefit was that my understanding of my mom and my respect for her grew in significant ways.

I've known others who have reached out to cousins, older siblings, aunts, uncles, and even old family friends to learn about their parents' and grandparents' generations. If you have gaps in your knowledge as I did, or even if you don't think you have gaps, take some time to talk with people who can shed more light on your family story. You'll be surprised what you'll learn by hearing stories from different perspectives, and you'll be glad you invested the time to explore.

Descriptors fall into five big categories:

1. Characteristics
2. Events
3. Roles
4. Issues
5. Values

We'll work through the categories one at a time. Each begins with a definition and a list of example words to give you a sense of the descriptors others have used in each category. However, you aren't limited to just these words. The examples are simply meant to be a catalyst for your thinking. Be precise and candid as you choose descriptive words that best capture the essence—both positive and negative—of the people and relationships in your genogram.

As you read through the five categories, label the shapes in your genogram with the corresponding descriptors.

**1. Characteristics:** Consistent traits or patterns of behavior.

- High/low nurture
- High/low achieving
- Secretive
- Deceptive
- Honest
- Gentle
- Quiet
- Abusive
- Faithful
- Spiritual
- Stable
- Present
- Distant
- Attention-seeking
- Controlling
- Funny
- Patient or impatient
- Smart
- Impulsive
- Needy
- Frugal
- Lazy
- Kind
- Mean
- Codependent
- Hardworking
- Poor boundaries
- Resilient
- Sickly
- People person
- Life of the party

What two or three words would you choose to describe the characteristics of each person on your genogram? Be sure to capture both strengths and weaknesses. Write those words above each person's name on your genogram. I find it helpful to use different colors for positive and negative traits; for example, green for positive traits and red for negative ones.

**2. Events:** Significant changes, events, or shifts in your family that shaped or altered the trajectory of you or someone else in your genogram.

- Natural disasters
- Spiritual milestones
- Illness or injury
- Relational fractures (divorce, disowning)
- Educational or vocational achievements
- Extramarital affairs
- Criminal activity
- Death (family member or loved one)
- Significant loss
- Moving
- Job change
- Incarceration
- Financial crisis

Many of us can name a handful of specific events in our family history that indelibly changed the course of our family's lives. The impact of these events could be positive or negative. An example from my childhood was our family's move from California to Washington State just as I was entering high school. This move changed the trajectory of my family in both positive and negative ways. A life-altering event in my adult life was the death of our middle daughter when she was nineteen.

For individuals, events might include winning an election, battling a significant illness, having a religious conversion, or owning an all-consuming business. For families, events might include losing a home to a fire or flood, a season of increased wealth or poverty, or spending substantial time in another country.

What life-altering events have you experienced in your immediate family? What life-altering events were experienced by previous generations in your family? Use green to write down events that had a positive impact and red for those that had a negative impact.

**3. Roles:** Relational roles that were assigned (and then acted out) within a family system.

- Victim
- Bully
- Invisible
- Baby
- Black sheep
- Responsible adult
- Peacemaker
- Perfect child
- Counselor
- Scapegoat
- Hero
- Star
- Responsible one
- Clown
- Mediator
- Caretaker
- Benefactor
- Villain
- Slacker

We often assume specific roles within our families when we are young. These roles are part of how we (as individuals) and our families (as units) cope with the stresses and circumstances we encounter. For example, a child in a family with a chronically depressed father might become a clown or a caretaker in an effort to help ease the father's depression and thereby receive needed love and care from him. A child whose parents often fought might become a mediator or a perfect child to cope with the stress of living in a conflict-ridden home.

I've learned a lot about how roles function from a concept called *family systems theory*, which was developed in the 1950s by researcher and therapist Murray Bowen. He suggested that each of us is part of an interconnected family unit; therefore, when one member has a shift or issue, it impacts the entire family system. Imagine a mobile, the kind that hangs over a baby's crib. When any piece of the mobile is touched and set in motion, all the other pieces move as well. Within each family, each individual is tethered to some extent to others. As such, we really can't understand ourselves independent of the emotional unit from which we come and the role we played within it.

I commonly hear stories of families in which there was a clearly identified problem person, a hero or saint, a long-suffering parent, and so on. Each of these roles were faithfully played by individuals within the family when they were kids, but the role-playing didn't stop there. The roles we assume as kids often persist into adulthood and shape the families we generate.

A friend of mine, now in her fifties, is the oldest of four siblings. When she was growing up, her mom was a poorly functioning alcoholic and her dad was a quiet, distant man who worked long hours. From a very early age, my friend functioned as the primary parent for the entire household. Now, decades later, even though her siblings are all married and living on their own, she is still the first person anyone in the family calls when there is a problem. As a child, she took on the role of parent and responsible problem solver in her family, and it's a role she continues to have to this day.

Similarly, I recently met with a man in his midforties who was struggling in nearly every aspect of his life. His girlfriend had recently left him, he'd just been fired from another job, and he was behind on most of his bills. When I asked if there was anyone in his family he could turn to for support in this difficult time, his response broke my heart.

"Not really," he said. "My family has never had much time for me. I've always been the family screwup."

The man had been assigned this unfortunate role as a child as part of his broken family system, and he continues to live out this role as an adult. He is fulfilling the descriptor his parents gave him decades ago. It doesn't take much insight to see how this childhood descriptor continues to have a negative impact on his life as an adult.

What roles have individuals in your family played? Write them on your genogram.

**4. Issues:** Behaviors or recurring problems that have an adverse impact on an individual or family unit.

- Alcohol or substance abuse
- Spiritual abuse
- Eating disorders
- Addictions
- Sexual abuse

- Physical or emotional abuse
- Domestic violence
- Pornography
- Criminal activity
- Fundamentalism

Some behaviors have a particularly toxic impact on individuals and families. Sexual abuse, domestic violence, fundamentalism, and addictions can leave scars for generations. Because some of these problems are considered shameful and are often hidden or denied, it can be difficult to identify them as you go farther back in your family history. However, given the prevalence of these issues in the population at large, it's fair to say that tens of millions of people in the United States have been adversely impacted by one or more of these destructive patterns.[3] Statistically, that means it is more than likely your family has also been adversely affected by one of these damaging issues at some point in your family tree.

This reality struck home with me during the genogram team-building day I mentioned earlier. My wife, September, was on our team at that time. When it was her turn to present her genogram, I noticed something troubling. Several generations back, there was a male relative who had likely sexually abused his daughters and two of his granddaughters. September drew out the generations that followed from that man's square, a total of seven children and more than twenty grandchildren. Several of his descendants had labels indicating abuse and/or addiction, and *twenty* marriages had ended in divorce. Only six of the twenty-seven relatives had intact, original marriages, and several of those who'd been divorced had gone on to experience multiple divorces.

I had been married to September for decades by this time, but neither of us had recognized this pattern in her family until she drew out her genogram. Her genogram showed how the abusive actions of one character in her family tree many decades ago may have impacted the trajectory of her family's story in significant and, in some cases, heartbreaking ways.

The destructive patterns that flow from traumatic events can indeed be long-lasting and span generations. The genogram helps us identify and name such patterns. Only when we have identified generational problems can we begin to address them and write a new plot for ourselves and the generations that follow. This is how we can break destructive family cycles.

What issues have impacted individuals or families on your genogram? Write them down.

**5. Values:** Spoken or unspoken ways of relating to the things that matter most in life.

- Conflict
- Respect
- Food
- Money
- Fairness

- Secrecy
- Honesty
- Sex
- Work
- Play

- Nurture
- Affection
- Expressing emotions
- Discipline
- Charity/generosity
- Religion

- Education
- Serving others
- Gender roles
- Humor
- Work ethic

All families have values. Sometimes those values are spoken and intentional. Other times, they are unspoken and/or unintentional. My wife and I were intentional about fostering a family culture of honesty, learning, play, and hard work with our kids when they were growing up. These values and the resulting family culture positively formed and influenced our children's adult lives, and I believe they will positively influence their children's lives as well.

Looking back, however, we see that we unwittingly also created a few unnamed family-culture values that were less positive. One in particular is our tendency toward sarcasm. Our sarcastic sense of humor can be hurtful when we fail to temper it. This unnamed family value has left an often-negative contribution to our family culture (although, dang, our family is funny and we laugh a lot). On a more serious note, in my work overseeing a recovery program for several years, I've heard countless stories in which a family value of parties and celebrations unwittingly led to excessive alcohol consumption and eventually to struggles with alcohol or substance abuse or addiction.

Every family culture embodies both positive and negative values, whether spoken or unspoken. They might have to do with money, conflict, sexuality, gender roles, work ethic, or any number of other issues.

Whether they were lived out intentionally or unintentionally, what positive and negative values were active in the family units on your genogram? Write them down.

Below is an example of how the genogram could look for two generations in a family of five. Notice the positive descriptors are noted on the upper left of each person's shape and negative descriptors are on the upper right. Roles (good kid, bad kid, and peacemaker) are in italics, and events (house lost in a fire), values (strong work ethic), and family issues (violence from the parents toward the children) are marked in bold. For your genogram, consider using different ink colors or different colors of highlighters to note positive and negative characteristics, roles, issues, events, and values.

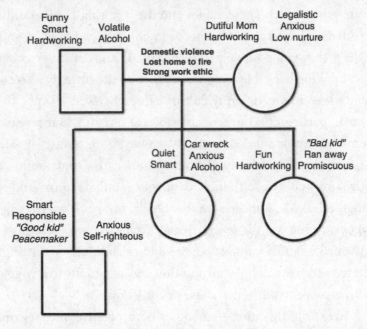

By this stage, the nuts and bolts of your genogram should be in place. Step back and admire your work! The rest of this chapter will help you extract information from your genogram that is vital to understanding your story.

## NOTICING THEMES

Let's review another basic genogram, this time for Jay, who has professional parents and one sibling, a younger sister.

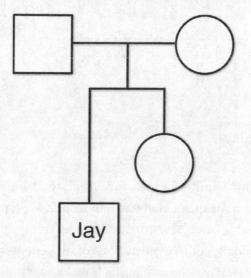

If we were to ask Jay to describe his parents, he would tell us that his dad was the second of six boys and his mother was the only girl in her family of four siblings. They married young and remained happily married until the death of his mother at an old age. Jay might add the following characteristics for the formative figures in his story:

**Father:** Hardworking, funny, low nurture, temper
**Mother:** Hardworking, smart, strong, low nurture

Can you see a theme starting to form?

What if we were to expand Jay's genogram to include his grandparents, aunts, and uncles? When he expands to a second generation, things get even more complicated.

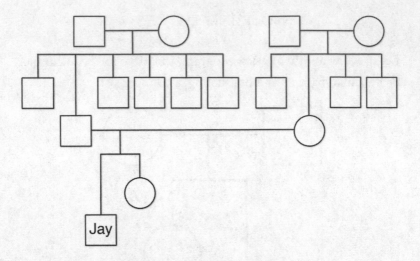

With this family tree structure in place, if Jay were to add descriptors to the major characters in his life, we'd notice "hard worker," "stern," and "low nurture" pop up frequently. They are themes throughout three generations of his genogram.

By now, you may be wondering how I know so many details related to this particular genogram. I know because Jay is a real person—my father.

When I add my mother's side, my genogram looks like this:

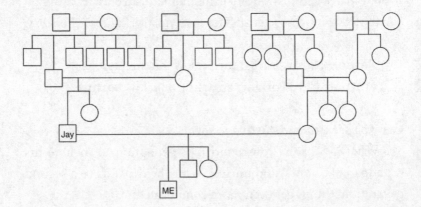

On my mother's side, the phrases "hard worker" and "low nurture" continue to be a surprisingly prevalent theme as well, perhaps because both my parents were raised by parents who lived through two world wars and the Great Depression.

This theme of hardworking, low-nurture adults struck me like a ton of bricks when I first discovered it about twenty years ago. I was in my thirties, and a seminary professor asked me to write out a genogram as a class assignment. Back then I was a cynic about exploring my story.

"C'mon," I protested, "I know my own family. I've heard all the stories. I lived through this. Why should I bother drawing it?"

"Trust me," he said. "You'll be surprised what you learn when you capture it on paper."

He was insistent, so I drew out my genogram. And he was right. This process was the catalyst that helped me understand and overcome many of the thought patterns that contributed to a repeated cycle of relational disappointment.

After I assembled the basic structure of my genogram (the squares, circles, and connecting lines), I wrote down descriptors for each of my relatives as best I could.

I was stunned by what I observed.

On the positive side, I noticed we are a family that earns its keep. People on both sides of the family are hard workers! I didn't realize how deeply a strong work ethic ran in my family until I drew this out. I had written "hard worker" on almost all of the squares and circles in my genogram. I felt proud of this part of my heritage. Other positive traits I noticed spanning from generation to generation included a good sense of humor, respect for learning, and an "I can figure it out" attitude.

On the negative side, I noticed a theme of control and

emotional distance. At the time, I had been married for almost twenty years and my marriage was not in a great place. As is often the case with marital distress, a number of factors contributed to our rough spot. When I looked at my genogram, one such factor struck me: my wife's irritating habit of telling me that I was controlling and emotionally detached. She didn't use the phrase "low nurture," but it was strongly implied in our arguments.

"You are so wrong," I protested whenever she raised the issue. "I'm not distant or controlling. I'm just focused. I may be a lot of things, but controlling is not one of them!"

I had no shelf on which to store any suggestion that I could be controlling or emotionally distant—until I reviewed my genogram. When I completed the genogram assignment, I sat stunned as I noticed how often I had written the words "low nurture," "distant," or "controlling" next to the adults who had helped form me. These were by far the most prominent themes in my entire genogram.

As I sat alone in my office and let those themes from my genogram sink in for the first time, I said out loud, "I *am* controlling and distant!" This realization—as obvious as it was to those closest to me—was nowhere on my radar until I drew out my genogram. Suffice it to say, this moment of insight was a major catalyst for me to finally take responsibility for my contributions to our marital troubles.

Notice the genogram did not create an excuse for me to blame my faults on my family. I was and am 100 percent responsible for my own behavior. Because my genogram mapped out all the people, values, and events that had shaped me, it helped me to understand where I learned to cope with the imperfections and disappointments of life the way I do.

My genogram exposed a story that now makes more sense to me. It is somehow easier to take responsibility for my faults when I understand that I came by them naturally, as did those in the generations before me.

Take some time now to stand back and look at your completed genogram. What are the major themes you notice? Circle the repetitive or closely related words you've written from generation to generation—both positive and negative. If you spot more than one theme, consider using a different color pen to mark each theme. Which traits show up in your own life and in your relationships today?

Congratulations! You completed your genogram. This document will serve you well moving forward. You can refer to it to help you understand how your past (even the years before you were born) created the cultural environment that formed you, influencing how you see yourself, the world, and your place in it.

Keep this document handy as you continue reading. You'll gather even more data to add to your genogram in the coming chapters.

## For Reflection

Spend some time reflecting on the questions on the next page by journaling your responses. Then, if you are comfortable, share your observations with someone who is safe and trustworthy (a close friend, a therapist, or a significant other).

- What are the highs and lows of your family story?
- What characteristics, events, roles, issues, and values have had the most influence on you?
- What parts of your genogram leave you feeling the most grateful?
- What insights did you gain into your own story? Into how you relate to others?
- How did the influence of previous generations make you a better person?
- What are some of the regrettable characteristics you carry from your family story?

# FOUR

# Positive Plot Points: Maximizing
# the Best Parts of Your Story

*If history were taught in the form of stories, it
would never be forgotten.*

—Rudyard Kipling

I have a client (let's call her Sharon) who was raised in Texas
by a gentle pastor-father and a mother who was a schoolteacher.
Sharon's consistent story line when she recalls her childhood is
that the one thing she could always count on growing up was the
constancy of family. Her family gathered at the table every morning for breakfast and every evening for dinner. During these
meals they laughed, shared stories, and stayed caught up with
each other's lives. This input from her childhood contributed to
a belief that she holds to this day: "Family matters. In the end, it
is your family who will be by your side."

This deeply held belief influences how Sharon thinks and behaves to this day. Now in her forties, with a high-power executive job and three kids of her own, she has kept her family as her number-one priority, even when it has slowed her race to the top of the corporate ladder. "Family matters" is a powerful, positive consequence of her childhood in Sharon's life today.

You and I, like Sharon, have positive story lines and inputs that have contributed to our beliefs and positive behaviors as adults.

## INPUTS, BELIEFS, AND CONSEQUENCES

By chronicling the formative events of our early years, we can examine their impact, both positive and negative, on our lives and relationships today. This next exercise will equip you to examine your story through the lens of three elements: inputs, beliefs, and consequences. It will help you pinpoint where your past formed the parts of your worldview and characteristics that help you thrive in your emotional and relational world—or cause you to struggle.

### Inputs

Inputs are the formative events (large and small, positive and negative) that influence our adult values, decisions, and behaviors. They are the basic building blocks that comprise the foundation and framework of our stories. Each of our stories includes many inputs: events, exposures, interactions with people, different seasons, significant accomplishments, and other experiences that left a mark on us in some way. Recalling and capturing our inputs gives us clarity on how we came to interpret the world in the unique way we do.

## Beliefs

Beliefs (both positive and negative) are what develop from our inputs. Becoming aware of the beliefs that were generated from our inputs is how our stories become more than just a list of random things that happened to us. Louis Cozolino commented on this in *Why Therapy Works*: "In the absence of self-awareness, our story is a simple chronology of events and our judgments about them."[1]

Understanding our beliefs is important because our beliefs consciously and unconsciously guide how we relate to other people. In fact, it's so important that we'll devote most of our attention to beliefs as we explore the "Now what?" questions in part III.

## Consequences

Your beliefs impact all your adult choices and behaviors, both positively and negatively. As psychologist Daniel Taylor noted, your beliefs "have shaped how you see yourself, the world, and your place in it."[2]

If we brought the belief "I'm just a screwup" into adulthood from some of the inputs we received in childhood, we're likely to sabotage our relationships and every other area of our lives because we subconsciously expect to fail. If we brought the belief "I am a good friend" from our childhood inputs, we're much more likely to succeed in relationships because we believe we have what it takes to be a good friend. In both examples, it is beliefs that produce relational consequences: the actions, behaviors, and patterns we exhibit as we interact with others in our lives.

## THE INTERACTION OF INPUTS, BELIEFS, AND CONSEQUENCES

The relationship between inputs, beliefs, and consequences is that one leads to another as seen here:

This process was active throughout your formative years. Your genogram likely identified several threads running through your family story that affected who you are today. Some of those threads showed up as inputs, which led to beliefs, which then led to consequences. For example, if, during your childhood, your parents took you to serve with them at a soup kitchen twice a month, you may have developed a belief that "it's everyone's responsibility to help those less fortunate." This belief or worldview may then lead to a consequence that, as an adult, you are benevolent and sensitive toward charitable causes.

Your story is a mixture of both positive and negative inputs, beliefs, and consequences. Let's first examine positive inputs, beliefs, and consequences. Then, in the next chapter, we'll consider the negative expressions of each.

### Positive Inputs

Even if your story has been largely painful and difficult thus far, you have probably experienced at least some positive inputs in your past. Perhaps it was an after-school program that served as an oasis for you, a kind aunt or uncle who took an interest in you, or the elementary schoolteacher who believed in you. Maybe you can recall one class in high school that inspired your career dreams, the challenging sports season in which you struggled but prevailed, or a memorable weekend trip that built you up, strengthened your character, and made you feel proud of your resilience. All these inputs feed positively into your life as an adult.

Here are some examples of positive inputs in three categories: environment, individuals, and events.

### Positive environment
- A safe, stable home
- Loving, nurturing parents
- Hardworking family
- Good genes (naturally smart, athletic, or good-looking)
- Adequate finances (never worried materially)
- Healthy dialogues
- Age-appropriate expectations
- Access to good schools

### Positive individuals
- Teacher who took an interest in you and invested in you
- Coach who saw your potential and pushed you
- Relative who listened and protected you
- Neighbor who was a faithful, safe support and good listener
- Parent who encouraged curiosity and nurtured you
- Sibling who mentored and protected you

**Positive events**

- Taking a family trip to Africa that expanded your view of the world
- Overcoming adversity to win a sports championship
- Playing the lead role in the school musical
- Visiting your grandmother each summer
- Overhearing your teacher say nice things about you to another teacher
- Teaching yourself how to juggle in junior high school
- Watching a parent courageously persevere through a tough season

Formative inputs don't need to be monumental in size or scale to have a significant impact on your life. One of my most formative positive inputs took place when my first-grade teacher made an offhand comment to me while passing back a paper. "Scott, you're an amazing artist," she said. "I just love your drawings!" I wasn't a kid who was obsessed with art, but I'd been trying my hand at drawing cartoons. This compliment from my teacher gave me confidence in school to try new things.

One of my sons experienced a positive input in middle school that led to positive beliefs and consequences in his life. In sixth grade, he won a school spelling bee. Although he hadn't studied for it, he took first place for his entire school. In eighth grade, he entered the contest again, and this time he won the competition for the whole school district. Reigning as the Dundee Middle School spelling bee winner wasn't his ultimate dream. "Being known as the spelling bee champ in junior high is like being a winner and a loser at the same time!" he once quipped. Even though he downplayed his victory at the time, I noticed how it changed him. From the time he won his first spelling bee, he had more confidence in his intellectual gifts. That one positive input increased his belief in his smarts, which led to positive consequences in how he viewed himself and interacted with his peers.

## Positive Beliefs

Positive inputs contribute to the formation of positive beliefs. These beliefs become the operating system or the lens through which we understand ourselves, the world, and our place in it.

When he was growing up, my dad was a hard worker, and he taught his kids to work hard. He did a great job of teaching my brother and me how to build and fix things. He also had a great sense of humor. From those positive inputs, I developed a few important positive beliefs: "Hard work is how you make it in life," "If I try hard, I can probably solve this problem," and "Life and work can be hard, so it might as well be fun."

My mother provided an invaluably positive input in my life as well, which led to one of my most beloved beliefs. Mom read constantly. When we were young, she regularly took my brother and me to the library. Later, she often bought us books. From the inputs of her example and from the way she made sure my brother and I had access to books, I developed the belief "Knowledge matters" and "Reading is worthwhile and brings joy." Reading and learning is one of my greatest joys to this day, and I trace its roots to my mom.

Here are some examples of positive beliefs we might have about ourselves, the world, and our place in it.

**Positive beliefs about how we see ourselves**
- I'm smart.
- I'm funny.
- I'm careful and diligent.
- I'm healthy and strong.
- I have what it takes to be successful.
- I'm kind.
- I can make the world a better place.
- I have much to contribute.
- I am worthy to be respected.
- I am organized.
- I am reliable.

**Positive beliefs about how we see the world**
- People are basically good and trustworthy.
- God is good and cares about me.
- If I'm nice, others will be nice back.
- Blood is thicker than water. (Family is the most important relationship.)
- Treat others fairly and they will treat me fairly.
- The world rewards integrity.
- I can learn so much about life from other cultures.
- We reap what we sow.

**Positive beliefs about how we see our place in the world**
- It is always best to tell the truth.
- I can make a positive difference in the world.
- I'll be successful because I'm a hard worker.

- Treating others with generosity is the key to a happy life.
- I can expect to have safe, loyal friends and loved ones.
- I have the intellect necessary to pursue my career dreams.
- I have what it takes to be a good friend and spouse.
- If I try hard enough, I will succeed.
- It's okay to fail sometimes.
- I deserve to be listened to and seen.

Predicting what sorts of beliefs someone may take away from a particular input isn't always intuitive. For example, when my elementary teacher said I was a great artist, I took away the belief that I could be successful in trying new things. Another kid might have walked away with the belief "I'm creative" or "Taking risks is how you get approval and make it in life."

When our son won the spelling bee, the belief that stuck was "I have a sharp mind." Another kid might have won the spelling bee and entered adulthood with different beliefs: "Hard work pays off" or "I thrive under stress." Which belief we take from our positive inputs depends on our natural wiring and our relationship with the person who provided the input. As we examine our stories, it's important to look beyond our inputs and identify the specific beliefs we took from them.

## Positive Consequences

Positive inputs yield positive beliefs, which then contribute to positive consequences and behaviors. The positive consequences in our lives are the virtuous traits and patterns of living that help us relate well with others, cope well with adversity, and otherwise succeed in life. When I teach about these concepts in a workshop or coaching setting, I help participants identify their positive consequences by asking them to respond to the question "What's lovely about me?"

## PUTTING IT ALL TOGETHER

All of us possess positive traits (consequences), those innate strengths that help us thrive in life or in relationships. By examining our stories, we can follow the trail of each consequence to its source: each positive consequence is fueled by a corresponding worldview (belief), and these positive beliefs were formed through one or more events and sources (inputs).

To help you get clear on what's lovely about you and how you developed those positive traits (inputs leading to beliefs that result in consequences), let's look at some examples of this process. The tables on pages 69 and 70 demonstrate positive inputs, beliefs, and consequences for two different people from two different families. Notice that you can't necessarily predict which inputs generate positive beliefs in a particular individual. Similarly, two people can have similar positive inputs and walk away with very different beliefs or consequences.

### Arjun: Hardworking, Successful Parents + Advocating Uncle

Arjun is a second-generation Indian man whose parents were professionals who put in long hours excelling at work. Despite their hectic schedules, his parents consistently made time to serve under-resourced people in their community and brought Arjun and his three siblings with them whenever they volunteered. As was his family culture, Arjun worked hard and excelled in school, particularly in the subjects of art and literature. Arjun also had an uncle, Raza, who regularly affirmed and invested in him.

| ARJUN | | |
|---|---|---|
| Positive Inputs | Positive Beliefs | Positive Consequences |
| • Our family served at a downtown food kitchen every Christmas.<br>• My parents were hard workers.<br>• Uncle Raza gave me his stamp collection.<br>• My tenth-grade teacher said I was a gifted writer. | • I can make a difference in the world.<br>• I am a good person.<br>• I must work hard to be successful.<br>• Innovation and creativity are important parts of leadership.<br>• The world is worthy of my efforts.<br>• Serving others is good.<br>• If I devote myself to my tasks the world will be a better place. | • I am generous.<br>• I improve myself.<br>• I do my best.<br>• I take creative risks.<br>• I am successful. |

## Regina: Encouraging Parents + Close-Knit Family

After fifteen years of infertility and IVF treatments, Regina's mom became pregnant and gave birth to her, the only child of a loving mom and dad. Regina was the apple of her family's eye and received much attention, praise, and encouragement. Her extended family would gather often, and in these settings, Regina was always the youngest and most special.

| REGINA | | |
|---|---|---|
| **Positive Inputs** | **Positive Beliefs** | **Positive Consequences** |
| • Our family always had dinner together and played board games.<br>• Our extended family gathered every summer and Christmas.<br>• My parents were attentive to my needs.<br>• Grandma introduced me to vegetarianism. | • Your family will always be with you. They are the most important people in your life.<br>• I am worthy of being taken care of.<br>• You only have one body, so you should take very good care of it. | • I am family oriented.<br>• I am loyal.<br>• I am confident.<br>• I take care of my body. |

Everyone, even those with traumatic or painful childhood stories, has at least a handful of positive inputs from their story, which foster positive beliefs and consequences in their adult lives. In order to understand and heal our stories holistically, it is essential that we gain clarity on our unique positive inputs, beliefs, and consequences. Embracing our positives provides the critical balance necessary when it comes time to put our entire story together (described in part III). It also helps us keep an accurate perspective as we delve into the negative parts of our stories in the next chapter. Let's take a look at your positives.

## IDENTIFYING YOUR POSITIVE INPUTS, BELIEFS, AND CONSEQUENCES

What are some of the positive inputs and beliefs from your story? What relationally productive consequences have you experienced as a result? Draw a three-column chart on a piece of paper or use the chart below to capture some of the positive elements from your story.

| YOU | | |
|---|---|---|
| Positive Inputs | Positive Beliefs | Positive Consequences |
| (from your childhood environment, individuals, and events) | (about yourself, the world, and your place in it) | (how you function in life and in your relationships) |
| | | |

It's both affirming and rewarding to chronicle the positive inputs and beliefs from your story. Those are happy memories. As you named some of the resulting admirable consequences in your life, I hope you felt a sense of healthy pride about the strengths with which you engage the world. I hope you also felt a ton of gratitude for the people, circumstances, and influences in your life that guided and formed you along the way.

While I would love to linger in the glow of the positive, there is much more to our stories. It's time to move on to the rest of the story—the negative plot points—to continue our trek to the life we want. Fasten your seat belt!

## For Reflection

Spend some time reflecting on the questions below by journaling your responses. Then, if you are comfortable, share your observations with someone who is safe and trustworthy (a close friend, a therapist, or a significant other).

- What connections did you identify between your positive inputs and the way you see the world?
- What positive consequences impact how you relate to others?
- To whom might you express gratitude for their influence in shaping who you are today? Do something tangible to thank them. Write a note or an email, make a call, perform an act of service, or send a small gift.

# FIVE

# Negative Plot Points: Healing the Hard Parts of Your Story

All sorrows can be borne if you put them into a story or tell a story about them.

—Isak Dinesen, *Out of Africa*

I first met Christopher when the HR director of his company reached out to me about coaching him after his third consecutive, negative quarterly review. Christopher had been a competent manager during his tenure in regional sales. The trouble started when he was promoted to corporate headquarters as vice president of sales. With Christopher's blessing, I spent time interviewing his boss, peers, and direct reports, and the insights they gave were consistent. On the positive side, they all described him as nice and cooperative. But they also occasionally experienced him as distant, vacant, and aloof. He was not connecting with any of the staff at corporate headquarters. When I asked him about this in our first meeting, he replied, "I don't know what they're talking about! I'm friendly to everyone. We chat all the time."

As we got to know each other better, he shared that he didn't connect on a deeper level with people outside work either. "Nice but distant" were words his few friends used to describe him. Christopher didn't understand the feedback, because this was the only type of relationship he had ever known.

Then he began to describe the environment in which he grew up as the youngest of three siblings. Things became clearer as I listened to him share his story. His father abandoned the family when Christopher was four years old, never to return or make contact. His mother worked two jobs to make ends meet, and when he was nine years old, she fell asleep behind the wheel of her car while driving home from a night shift and hit a tree. She was killed instantly. Christopher and his older siblings were sent to live with their elderly grandparents.

One by one, his older siblings left home early to make a life for themselves. Then his eighty-six-year-old grandfather died. The repetitive experience of abandonment and loss left Christopher with a subconscious belief about the world: "Don't get attached to anyone, because they will always leave you."

Christopher was not consciously aware he held this worldview, but it was clearly present subconsciously, and it led to significant negative consequences throughout his adult life. He was a loner. And while he was aware of his loneliness, he readily chose to keep his distance from others rather than risk the inevitable pain of betrayal and abandonment.

# NEGATIVE INPUTS, BELIEFS, AND CONSEQUENCES

If the positive plot points were the whole of our stories, the world would be a much happier place (and you would have no need for this book). Sadly, for each of us, there is another side to our stories, a side we must explore if we want to do the rest of our lives better.

As we begin to explore the negative elements of our stories, it's important to remember that this is not an exercise in blame, a chance to make excuses for our mistakes, or an opportunity to assign fault to other people or bad circumstances. Instead, as we explore this more difficult layer, our motivation is to gain insight into our past so we can expose the root of some of the unhelpful relational patterns that hinder us in adulthood. We want to equip ourselves to do our own work and grow where we need to grow.

We want to do the rest of our lives better and move toward living the life we really want. But we can't get where we want to go until we are clear on where we've been. And understanding the negative plot points in our stories is vital to getting clear on where we've been. This was the journey Christopher began in my office to heal the wounds of his past. The first step was to get clear on the negative inputs that contributed to his view of himself and the world in which he lived.

## Negative Inputs

No matter how great our stories may have been, no matter how awesome our childhood was, and no matter how hard our parents tried to provide us with only positive inputs, each of us has experienced negative inputs. We have all had damaging experiences and been exposed to negative environments that adversely affected our capacity to engage others in adulthood. As a result, we all carry some wounds.

Some of our negative inputs are dramatic and embedded in us a primal shame or fear and possibly left us with post-traumatic stress. Survey data suggest that in a group of one hundred adults, at least twenty will have experienced explicit sexual harm as children. An even greater number will have suffered physical abuse, and greater numbers still will have experienced emotional, verbal, and/or spiritual abuse.

Many of us grew up in environments characterized by rigid black-and-white thinking. This is true of those raised in homes that perpetuated racial prejudice or religious extremism or fundamentalism. Such environments often produce adults who carry deeply negative consequences (prejudice or intolerance) that can be socially harmful for generations.

Many negative inputs might have been beyond our control. For example, we may have experienced calamity as a child when a car accident injured or killed a family member or a house fire destroyed our family's possessions. Or we may have inherited physical traits that left us with negative inputs: we were too short, too tall, too heavy, or too thin. Maybe we had funny hair, bad acne, a big nose, crooked teeth, or ears that stuck out. Perhaps we weren't athletic or struggled academically. These are things over which we had no control, but they may have caused lingering emotional wounds.

For others, negative inputs may have come in the form of physical ailments, mental illness, or financial strain. Some of us grew up in homes with addicted, impaired, or absent parents and ended up parenting our siblings. Some of us were even thrust into parental roles with our own parents. And even more of us grew up in homes that experienced the chaos of divorce. Such negative inputs rarely leave a child unscathed.

If you search your story and don't find any dramatic traumas or stories of significant harm, that's okay. Identifying your negative inputs isn't an exercise of listing the worst things that ever happened to you. In fact, there may be some less traumatic events that don't necessarily register as significant negative inputs. Similarly, not all negative inputs are the result of trauma, abuse, or tragic circumstances. Sometimes the negative inputs that caused the most harm don't look very dramatic on paper. One careless and hurtful comment by a parent, coach, friend, or teacher might have pierced you and left a lasting adverse impact. It might have seemed small to others, but it wounded you deeply.

Negative nicknames or roles assigned to you by your parents often cause lasting harm. Perhaps your parents jokingly called you the problem child when you were young. That characterization stuck with you through the years: your siblings could do no wrong, but you seemed to never get it right. Or perhaps you were your parents' chosen one who could do no wrong. This role carried with it the expectation that you please your parents and make them proud, but it also brought jealousy and contempt from your siblings. The golden child scenario is an ancient one. Think of Andrew Lloyd Webber's *Joseph and the Amazing Technicolor Dream Coat*, a retelling of the biblical story of Jacob and Joseph, his favorite son. Joseph's older brothers retaliated against their favored brother by throwing him into a pit, and then selling him into slavery, after which he languished in a prison cell for years. Being the favorite child often comes at a cost.

If I were to walk you through my childhood story, you'd hear some significant negative experiences that might sound dramatic, and yet many of them didn't necessarily create a lasting negative impact. On the flip side, I can recall a number of incidents that, from the outside, seem like no big deal. But those small wounds had a disproportionately large negative impact on me, one that distorted my beliefs about myself well into adulthood.

When I was in fourth grade, I tried out for a Little League baseball team. Up to that point, I had done all right as a player in my low-pressure district softball league. Because I was a left-hander who could throw hard, a coach from one of the upper-level teams drafted me in hopes of making me a star pitcher, even though I had never thrown a hardball.

It turned out I was neither a good pitcher nor a good baseball player. I quickly became overwhelmed by my highly skilled teammates, many of whom were two grades older than me. I ended up hating baseball, and the more my attitude sank, the worse I got at the game. Soon it was clear to everyone that I was a liability for the team, but the coach was obliged to play me for at least two innings of every game.

In the big scheme of things, this season was a pretty normal episode in the life of a young boy. But because I was a sensitive kid, that exposure created a number of negative inputs in my story. I took away the belief that failing at something is the worst thing that can happen. In adulthood, that belief led to a fear of failure or of looking stupid—a negative consequence I continue to navigate to this day.

Another event that left a disproportionately large negative

impact happened when I was in fifth grade. My father had just finished building our house by hand—an impressive feat—and he was rightly proud of the outcome. He invited a bunch of our relatives over, and I was excited because such gatherings were rare for our family. Everyone arrived and was chatting together in the living room. I took a risk and made a funny comment, which was unusual, given that I was introverted by nature.

My dad looked over at me with disgust and rolled his eyes. Then he said, voice dripping with sarcasm, "Oh, that's *so* funny, Scott. Just be quiet."

I was mortified.

I'm now in my midfifties, and I still get a pit in my stomach from those awful feelings of embarrassment and shame. It's entirely possible that impartial witnesses would have interpreted these events differently and would be surprised by the negative impact they had on me. This makes sense, because the witnesses aren't me. They aren't wired like me. They didn't live the story I'd lived before these events took place. Their interpretation might be valid, but so is mine.

Whether or not an event *should* have had a negative impact is not relevant. I'm not looking to justify how I was impacted. I'm not looking to assign blame. I'm simply seeking to understand the negative impact of each event so I can concentrate on repairing the resulting distorted beliefs and consequences.

You, too, have stories that left their marks on you, distorting your beliefs about yourself, the world, and your place in it. Whether large or small, what experiences from your growing-up years created negative inputs in your life? Here are some examples of negative inputs in three categories: environment, individuals, and events.

## Negative environment
- Unsafe or unstable home
- Little nurture from parents or caregivers
- Parent(s) overidentified by career
- Lack of athleticism, smarts, beauty, etc.
- Poverty
- Poor educational opportunities
- Racist, fundamentalist, or black-and-white thinking
- Family environment with secrets and hiding
- Extreme ideology
- Favoritism or rejection by a parent or caregiver
- Parent overly concerned about what others thought (appearances)

## Negative individuals
- Teacher who criticized you
- Coach who shamed you
- Relative who abused you
- Parent who was addicted or absent
- Parents who divorced
- Parent who was neglectful
- Neighbor/schoolmate who bullied you
- Religious authority figure who harmed or exploited you

## Negative events
- Natural disaster that wiped out your family's possessions
- Incidents of abuse (particularly by someone you trusted)
- Divorce
- Abandonment by a parent
- Death of a parent or sibling

- Significant illness or physical disability
- Failing to make a sports team, get a role in the school play, win a class election, or other disappointments
- Experience of embarrassment or humiliation

It's vitally important to identify the key negative inputs in your story, because those inputs led to distorted beliefs, which are key contributors to the relational challenges you may be experiencing today.

## Negative Beliefs

Our negative inputs distort our beliefs about ourselves, the world, and our place in it. These inaccurate and misleading beliefs begin to form early in our lives, but as kids we don't recognize they are distortions. Instead, we create narratives to try to make sense of them; for example, "Mommy and Daddy got divorced because I was bad" or "I'm not attractive enough to be loved." Social psychologist Arthur W. Frank described how we carry the beliefs we grow up with and how they guide us "powerfully but not well."[1] Social scholar Timothy D. Wilson described these beliefs as *core narratives*. "People have core narratives about relationships that are rooted in their early interactions with their primary caregivers," he noted, "and these narratives act as filters, influencing interpretations of their adult relationships—sometimes in unhealthy ways."[2]

These negative beliefs, like their positive counterparts, significantly impact our relationships and, in this case, hinder our ability to thrive. Only when we develop an accurate understanding of our negative beliefs can we begin to change—and heal—our unproductive relational patterns.

My friend Andy Hartman is a gifted psychologist who has spent thirty years helping clients unpack the negative beliefs and distortions that come from the negative inputs of their early years. He refers to these distorted beliefs as *messages of the wound*. This term helps us understand the specific ways our past can distort how we see ourselves, the world, and our place in it. Hartman also notes that sometimes a message of the wound can be more traumatic than the event itself because its impact is ongoing.

Because these wounds happen to us in our formative years, we're often unaware of the resulting negative beliefs (messages of the wound). The distortions feel normal to us because they became part of our lives before we were old enough to challenge their validity. As adults, we're often shocked when we discover how our relational patterns and behaviors have been so adversely influenced by subconscious and distorted views of ourselves, the world, and our place in it.

Our messages of the wound contribute, often substantially, to the operating system through which we filter our life experiences and our interactions with other people. Because these messages have always been part of our thinking, they're hard to notice as unusual or unhelpful, which is unfortunate, because shedding these messages is essential to doing the rest of our lives better.

Here are some examples of negative beliefs (messages of the wound) we might have about ourselves, the world, and our place in it.

### Negative beliefs about how we see ourselves
- I am responsible for the happiness of others.
- I can't be myself.
- I can do no wrong.

- My feelings don't matter.
- My value comes from being perfect and performing well.
- I am bad, the black sheep, the screwup.
- My type is superior/inferior to all others.
- I am not good at relationships.
- It's the job of my parent (friend, spouse, etc.) to meet my needs.

## Negative beliefs about how we see the world
- God is mad at me.
- Relational intimacy is not safe and always causes pain.
- Those who are a certain gender (ethnicity, vocation, etc.) are more/less important in society.
- The world is not safe. It's a dog-eat-dog world.
- Conflict is bad.
- Intense feelings are dangerous and unwelcome.
- Men/women cannot be trusted.
- Anger is hurtful and should be avoided.
- Nice guys finish last.
- Others should sacrifice to make me happy.

## Negative beliefs about how we see our place in the world
- No one will protect me. I must look out for myself.
- I must find someone to take care of me.
- We must hide our problems and put on a happy face.
- My needs are secondary to those of others.
- Life is not worth living if there isn't a man/woman in my life.
- People will betray you.

- It is my job to solve other people's problems.
- If I disagree with or disappoint others, they will leave me.
- My feelings will overwhelm other people.
- Eventually, I will be abandoned. It's only a matter of time.
- Only whiners talk about their problems.
- If I tell the truth, people will leave me.
- My purpose and goals in life matter more than the goals or purposes of other people.

Discerning the specific, unique messages of the wound that have developed in your life can be tricky, because they aren't always intuitive. They can't be predicted based solely on what happened to you in the past. Instead, they are the result of two components: what happened to you, *plus* your unique temperament and personality. For example, my younger brother and I share most of the same negative inputs from our childhoods. We grew up in the same environment with the same set of parents. But our negative beliefs—and the coping mechanisms and negative consequences each of us developed to navigate life— could not be more different. This is quite common in families because no two siblings are exactly alike and parents have unique relationships with each child.

Let's consider three family scenarios to better understand how multiple negative beliefs (messages of the wound) can be generated within one household.

### Family 1: The Unsafe Family

This family is comprised of a mother, a father, two sons, and two daughters. The father is an angry man. In fact, Dad is the only one in the family who's allowed to be angry. His voice is also the only voice that matters; his word is law and it is final. If the kids cross him, they're likely to get backhanded or at least receive a verbal lashing. Meanwhile, Mom is aloof and distant. She neither challenges her husband nor protects the kids.

Growing up in this household, all four children are exposed to the same negative inputs. As a result, they may develop similar messages of the wound. However, it's more likely that each of them will enter adulthood with different stories and messages of the wound based on their natural wiring, temperaments, specific circumstances, and the unique relationships they shared with each parent.

Here are some examples of the messages of the wound these children might take into adulthood. Notice how these messages could apply to any child, regardless of gender or birth order.

- It's just best to stay small and keep quiet. Don't make a fuss.
- The man of the house is the only one allowed to express anger.
- My needs and thoughts aren't important.
- Family unity is not important.
- My voice doesn't matter.
- No one will protect me.
- Anger and intimidation are the best way to influence people.

As adults, these messages inevitably lead to negative consequences in how each sibling navigates relationships. Perhaps one of the children will grow into an angry spouse and parent like Dad. Another child may avoid conflict at all costs, managing his or her resentment at having no voice by self-medicating with alcohol. Still another might become a hyperdefensive spouse and coworker. The possible negative consequences are endlessly diverse, depending on how each sibling interpreted the messages of the wound that came their way. What the siblings have in common is this: none will enter adulthood *without* some negative consequences from a childhood riddled with negative messages of the wound.

## *Family 2: The Secretive Family*

This family is comprised of a mother, a father, a twelve-year-old son, and a ten-year-old daughter. On the surface they look like a happy, small-town, all-American family. But behind closed doors, everything looks different. The kids face the wrath of their mother, whose spontaneous outbursts of rage frighten everyone in the family, including their father, who has learned to avoid his wife's fury by slipping into his study as soon as he gets home from work. In the secrecy of his study, he escapes into a world of sexual conversation and gratification from people he meets in internet chat rooms.

Meanwhile, the kids are left unprotected, forced to navigate Mom's anger on their own. They band together and make every effort to stay away from the drama of their home. Afternoons are the hardest, and they've learned that offering Mom a glass of wine with dinner seems to calm her down. Mom spends the rest of the evening refilling her glass to de-escalate her rage. In public, the kids know to put on happy faces and behave as if all is well at home. From early childhood, both parents drilled into them the importance of protecting the family's image. There's a lot at stake, because Dad is the pastor of the small community church and Mom is a well-known community activist who is running for mayor.

Here are some examples of the messages of the wound these kids might bring into adulthood:

- Image is primary. We must hide our problems.
- Put on a happy face and don't tell the truth.
- I am alone in this world.
- My value comes when I'm perfect, because that's what the world needs to see.
- Marriage is dangerous.
- Drinking calms my nerves.
- My role in the world is to not make waves.
- If the world knew the truth about me, I'd be rejected.
- What the world doesn't know won't hurt them. Telling the truth is optional.
- Isolation is the way to stay safe.
- The world is not safe.

A child growing up in this environment will use these distorted narratives to make sense of the world and provide a way to navigate what they believe is a pervasively conflicted and unsafe world for the rest of their life.

## *Family 3: The Conflicted Family*

This couple has been married for fifteen years and has a six-year-old daughter. Because of some vocational setbacks, the family's financial picture is bleak. As a result, the parents' relationship is rocky and volatile. They fight often, and their fights are loud and contemptuous. They have separated and reconciled several times in recent years.

Their daughter finds herself caught in the middle. Through

her young eyes, it seems like family time means trying to calm the storm between her parents. When they fight, Dad stonewalls, refusing to speak with Mom, who then resorts to yelling, crying, and pouting to get Dad to reengage. This insightful girl notices that her parents seem to hate each other more when it's just the two of them in a room, but when she walks in, they become civil and polite. From her earliest memories, she has learned to play the role of peacekeeper. Now at age six, she lives under the intense, unspoken pressure of being the one responsible for holding her family together.

Here are some examples of the messages of the wound this child might take into adulthood:

- The happiness of others is my responsibility.
- If you want your way, just scream and cry.
- It is best to avoid conflict at all costs.
- Being financially secure is all that matters.
- I can get my way by being charming.
- I am responsible for the feelings of others.
- Intense feelings are dangerous.
- Using pouting, guilt, and tears gets others to pay attention to you.
- Marriage is misery.
- My needs are secondary. It's my job to look after others.

From these examples, you notice that the messages of the wound are both individual and unique. The messages that inform the decisions of our adult lives are always present, but they are not always intuitive or obvious. It's worth taking the time to discern your own messages of the wound, because the distorted beliefs from those negative inputs in your story have a profound influence on your adult patterns of behavior and relationships. This comes as no surprise. Since each of us enters adulthood with a handful of distorted views of ourselves, the world, and our place in it, we are left with an ache of dissatisfaction that we manage in any number of unproductive ways, all in an effort to make sense of the lies we believe to be true.

## Negative Consequences

Our distorted beliefs (messages of the wound) alter how we see the world and make substantial contributions to the negative consequences in our relationships. Negative consequences are the conscious and unconscious means by which we try to either numb or outrun the ache we feel.

Here are some examples of negative consequences:

- Drinking too much
- Telling lies to hide shortcomings
- Defensiveness; inability to take criticism
- Focusing only on one's own needs
- Feeling the need to fix others
- Ignoring one's needs and serving others
- Inability to trust others, resulting in feelings of isolation and loneliness
- Whining
- Playing the victim card
- Bitterness
- Self-righteousness
- Inability to bond well with others
- People pleasing
- Anger problems
- Inability to speak up
- Using food for comfort
- Numbing with social media, video games, etc.
- Controlling and/or nagging others

- Overidentifying with one's work; therefore, working all the time
- Lacking resilience when life is hard
- Refusing to ask for help out of a fear of being needy
- Lacking clear core values that guide one's life
- Settling for the false intimacy of porn
- Perfectionism
- Pessimism
- Feeling entitled and self-absorbed
- Making poor sexual decisions
- Choosing poor romantic partners

Change is hard. For most of us, it's only when our negative consequences result in relational strain or vocational problems that we seek help. We enter counseling, sign up for marriage workshops, or buy books (like this one) dealing with family-of-origin issues, because we're motivated to relieve the pain of our negative consequence patterns.

## INPUTS THAT ARE BOTH POSITIVE *AND* NEGATIVE

Not all of our inputs can be neatly categorized as either positive or negative. Sometimes our more complex situations contribute to both positive and negative beliefs.

Most of us can recall an adverse circumstance from our youth that was painful but also made us stronger. My friend Marie grew up as the oldest child of a violent, alcoholic father and a passive, codependent mother. Her story is an example of how someone's negative inputs can lead to both positive and negative beliefs and consequences.

Marie was often thrust into the role of parent and protector of her younger brother and sometimes their mother as well. Her childhood was riddled with dramatic and dangerous negative inputs that resulted in negative beliefs and consequences in her adult life. Marie struggles with insecurities around performance and value that, at times, have hindered her relationally and vocationally.

And yet Marie has also mined from these negative inputs some significant positive beliefs about herself, the world, and her place in it. She believes she is a powerful person (and I agree), that her voice matters, and that she can make a positive difference in the world. The positive relational consequences of her positive beliefs are impressive. She is one of the best mothers and best pastors I know. She's also one of the funniest and most delightful people my wife and I have ever met. All this despite a profoundly painful childhood.

Conversely, our seemingly positive inputs can sometimes contribute to negative beliefs. I mentioned earlier how my dad's expectation of "hard work done right" instilled some significant positive beliefs and consequences in my brother and me, for which I am deeply grateful. Dad's high expectations consumed an inordinate percentage of my childhood and teen hours as my brother and I helped him build a house and a barn, tended a menagerie of farm animals, worked in his many side businesses, and assisted with the heavy-duty chores on our 110-acre farm. These years of hard work taught my brother and me innumerable positive and practical skills that continue to benefit us in adulthood.

But they also left behind some negative messages. I carried into adulthood the belief that my only value to others is what I can produce for them. Another distorted message is that tasks are more important than relationships. The vocational overdrive in me has at times adversely affected my relationships. Undoubtedly, this distortion impacts my roles as a spouse and a dad. By identifying the negative beliefs (messages of the wound) I took from childhood, I've been able to mine the beauty of those inputs and take steps to heal the distorted beliefs they left behind.

Both positive and negative inputs are plot points in our stories that have the power to cause either positive or negative consequences in our lives—and often both.

## PUTTING IT ALL TOGETHER

The most helpful insights you'll gain to heal your broken stories and improve your relationships come from a deeper understanding of the negative parts of your story. To get clear on these types of insights, we need to be honest with ourselves about the negative consequences we currently experience, as well as the negative inputs and beliefs that led to those consequences. A candid assessment helps us understand our unique messages of the wound. To better prepare you for assessing the negative plot points in your story, let's revisit the stories of Arjun and Regina from the previous chapter.

### Arjun: Busy/Absent Parents + Bullying Brother

When we captured the positive side of Arjun's story in the last chapter, we learned that his parents were professionals who put in long hours but still found time to contribute to their community by volunteering. Let's look at the flip side of the story: the adverse impact of Arjun's family culture.

Because of their long hours, neither of Arjun's parents were home much during the bulk of his childhood. As a result, Arjun had to figure out life on his own. More problematic for him was his older brother, who bullied, manipulated, and physically accosted him at every opportunity. Arjun's checked-out parents didn't notice the bullying, and when he asked them for protection, they told him to just work it out. Without the protection that a parent should provide, Arjun grew up in an environment of constant chaos and fear at home. Now in his forties, Arjun is a rising executive in a small company where he is verbally abused by his boss. Many of his peers underperform and expect Arjun to pick up the slack. *Just work it out*, Arjun tells himself.

Things aren't much better in Arjun's personal life. His wife and two teenage children contribute little to the functioning, cleaning, or maintenance of the household, leaving Arjun feeling resentful and overworked. His only respite comes from ending his evenings with hours of cruising social media.

| ARJUN | | |
|---|---|---|
| Negative Inputs | Negative Beliefs | Negative Consequences |
| • Busy, distant, distracted parents<br>• Lonely childhood<br>• Bullying brother | • I am not worth protecting.<br>• No one will notice my needs.<br>• The world is cruel and unfair.<br>• I deserve a life of mistreatment. | • I am codependent.<br>• I don't advocate for myself.<br>• I avoid conflict at all costs.<br>• I feel sorry for myself. |

## Regina: Overindulgent Parents

As you may recall from the last chapter, Regina was born as the prized only child to older parents. It turns out this also translated into a home with no boundaries or limits.

Regina's parents were overindulgent throughout her childhood, and as a result, she grew up as the classic spoiled child. Whenever Regina pouted or threw a tantrum, her parents stopped everything to give her whatever she wanted.

This dynamic worked pretty well for Regina until she was in high school and discovered that her pouting and tantrums didn't work well with her peers or teachers. She had little resilience for facing adversity or conflict. She couldn't handle the structure and demands of sports, extracurricular activities, or mutually satisfying relationships. Her only friendships were with codependent people who gave in to her demands, people who didn't mind that everything had to revolve around her, or with people who used Regina for her money.

Things got worse when Regina went to college. No one had any patience for this spoiled, demanding young woman. She burned through a number of roommates in her freshman dorm, and by the start of her sophomore year, no one wanted to room with her. She was all alone.

Regina is now thirty years old, and this pattern hasn't changed. She expects romantic partners to cater to her every whim, even though she makes little effort to serve them or give back. As a result, Regina is single and lonely. She is convinced the world has somehow missed her brilliance and value. She feels the world has wronged her, and she spends her days with increasing bitterness and intolerance of others.

| REGINA | | |
|---|---|---|
| Negative Inputs | Negative Beliefs | Negative Consequences |
| • Overindulgent parents<br>• No opportunities to develop resilience or self-sacrifice | • I am the most important person in the world.<br>• Life should be comfortable.<br>• Throwing a fit gets you what you want.<br>• Others should give in to my desires.<br>• If you want something, take it! | • Selfish, self-absorbed<br>• Lacks resilience<br>• Lacks skills to get along with others<br>• Lonely and alone |

As you can see from the two examples above, sometimes similar inputs from the same sources can lead to different messages and consequences. In Arjun's case, his parents were both hardworking (a positive input) and distant (a negative input). With Regina, her parents were both devoted (a positive input) and indulgent (a negative input). This is true for all of us. Even the most loving parents still miss the mark in some ways. And even the most painful childhood still holds hints of beauty along the way.

Mining our stories for negative inputs goes against our sense of loyalty to our parents and our childhood. It can be frightening to admit everything wasn't perfect. That's normal. Remember, we want to be clear on our stories not to blame others but to understand ourselves.

For the sake of clarity on how the negative side of the equation can be more difficult, let's look at two more examples.

## Lucia: Stay-at-Home Mom + Absent Dad

Lucia was raised in a home with a stay-at-home mom and a father who traveled extensively for work. With her father out of town up to four days a week, her mother resented being a single parent to Lucia and her four younger siblings. By the time Lucia was in fifth grade, her mother dealt with her resentment by throwing herself into volunteer work at church and social engagements with friends. Lucia and her siblings often came home from school to an empty house. Because her mom was overcommitted to volunteer and social activities, Lucia often made lunches and dinners for her siblings on the days when Dad was out of town. By the time Lucia entered middle school, her siblings turned to her—rather than Mom—for nurture, help, and encouragement.

| LUCIA | | |
|---|---|---|
| Negative Inputs | Negative Beliefs | Negative Consequences |
| • Loss of childhood<br>• Too much responsibility at an early age<br>• Abandonment by mother (volunteerism and social engagements) and father (vocation) | • I am not worthy of being cared for or nurtured.<br>• The world only takes and never gives.<br>• Women belong at home.<br>• Men can't be relied upon.<br>• Parenting is a hands-off affair.<br>• The happiness and well-being of my family rests on my shoulders. | • Emotionally shut down<br>• Controlling<br>• Angry<br>• Over-responsible<br>• Codependent<br>• Uses alcohol to cope |

As an adult, Lucia spends all her time meeting the needs of her husband and children. These past few years, she has begun to relax a bit with several glasses of wine at the end of the day.

The most critical part of understanding the negative plot points in your story is identifying your negative beliefs, which means discerning your messages of the wound and putting them into words. It may sound straightforward, but it doesn't come easy for most of us. In fact, this typically requires quite a bit of time and thought, often aided by journaling and processing with others.

To give you an idea of how this happens, I want to share one more example. This one demonstrates how one of my coaching clients worked through the process of discerning her distorted messages of the wound. While yours will undoubtedly differ from hers, I hope that understanding how she gained clarity on her distorted message—and how that clarity greatly benefited her—will encourage you and give you an example to follow.

## Darcy: Critical, Perfectionistic Mother

Darcy was an executive vice president in a large company. Her boss, the CEO, asked me to coach her because she was a "great talent" who was nevertheless "leaving a wake of resentful colleagues behind her that has become impossible to ignore." Darcy was very critical of others. Her husband, direct reports, and coworkers took the brunt of her harsh rebukes.

In exploring her story, Darcy could easily identify the disapproval of her perfectionist mother as one of her negative inputs and her own intolerance of others as a negative consequence. But connecting the two with a negative belief was a struggle. The best she could come up with was "I guess I'm just like my mother. All the women on Mom's side of the family are perfectionists."

While it was true that she had probably learned to cope with her ache for acceptance and love the same way her mother had coped with *her* ache—through perfectionism—Darcy, like you and me, believed a distorted message about herself and her value that was contributing to the problem. Until she dug a little deeper to identify the *message* behind her ache, I knew she wouldn't be able to grow into a healthier person emotionally and relationally. "I'm just a perfectionist like my mom" wasn't so much a negative belief as it was an observation, and it barely scratched the surface of Darcy's ache. What was beneath it?

To identify her message of the wound, Darcy needed to connect the dots from her negative inputs to the consequences, in which her critical demeanor was damaging her personal and professional relationships. What were the coordinates that would help her gain clarity on her story so she could get where she wanted to go?

In our weekly conversations, we focused on identifying those coordinates. In essence, I asked her, "Where are you?"

Darcy's first pass at her message of the wound focused on defending her critical nature: "I shouldn't have to put up with stupid people." This statement was certainly true of how she reacted to the world, but it didn't explain her ache. "I shouldn't have to put up with stupid people" was an expression of her negative consequence (intolerance), but it didn't enlighten us about the distorted way Darcy saw herself, the world, or her place in it. She simply used this statement to legitimize her bad treatment of others.

We met for several months, exploring the link between her negative inputs (her demanding and critical mother) and her negative consequences (her critical nature toward others). I'll never forget the meeting when a light bulb turned on for Darcy. Her conclusions went something like this:

- "There are only two types of people in this world, the very best and the terrible," which reflected her distorted view of the world.
- "I am only worthy if I am the best," which reflected her distorted view of herself.

When she spoke those phrases out loud, a light bulb of understanding went on in Darcy's mind. Suddenly she saw why she behaved the way she did, and she was able to connect the next important dot.

"There is the best and there is the terrible, and I feel like the whole world must think I am terrible," she said. "And I'm so afraid that *I am* terrible." Then she quietly said, "I hate myself when I am terrible."

And there it was.

Darcy was only able to recognize her disabling terror and contempt for her imperfect parts when she explored the distorted messages of the wound. With that, the dam broke. Darcy wept tears of relief and compassion for herself. For the first time, she recognized that her critical behavior was rooted not merely in a family pattern—"All the women on Mom's side of the family are perfectionists"—but in a deep fear that her mother's relentless criticisms of her as a child had been right: she *was* terrible.

With clarity on how her message of the wound was the missing link between her negative inputs and negative consequences, Darcy began catching herself when she felt ashamed of her own imperfections or was tempted to lash out at someone for theirs. She reminded herself that the notion that people are either terrible or the best was a lie, and that a more accurate belief is that all of us are a mixture of beauty and brokenness. Then she was able to respond differently when someone frustrated her. She was well on the road to improving how she handles her relationships.

Did Darcy instantly become a warm and fuzzy person? Did all of her relationships instantly repair themselves? No. She still had work to do. But from that moment on, Darcy knew she was defining her problem more accurately. And because she had the correct diagnosis, she could finally begin a productive treatment plan. This allowed her to tackle her negative consequence of irritability at its root. Whenever she felt the tide of intolerance swell inside, instead of telling herself, "I'm so tired of stupid people," she coached herself with little phrases of self-talk to neutralize her messages of the wound:

- "I don't need to see this person as terrible to avoid feeling terrible myself."
- "Even this irritating person has some beautiful qualities."
- "The fact that I am smart does not make others stupid."
- "I don't need to make others pay for my own insecurities."
- "Making others feel terrible doesn't help me overcome my own fear of being terrible."

Over time, Darcy taught herself to react to disappointment in a more measured, productive manner. It's been a couple of years now since we finished our work together, but I still bump into her occasionally. It's fun to see her thrive as her relationships heal. She chose to do the hard work of really understanding her messages of the wound, and in doing so, she broke the long-established pattern passed down to her by generations of critical women. And her life is richer for it.

## YOUR NEGATIVE INPUTS, BELIEFS, AND CONSEQUENCES

Now it's your turn. Use the chart on the next page to capture your negative inputs, the resulting negative beliefs (messages of the wound), and the negative consequences that impact how you relate to others today. If, like Darcy, you struggle to name the most accurate messages of the wound from your story, then leave the middle column blank for now. Fill out the left and right columns first, then ponder the link between them. What distortion of reality contributes to your negative behavior? What fear resides in you from your earlier years that results in the destructive coping style you use as an adult? When Darcy got to the realization that her conduct was less about reacting to stupid people and more about a subconscious fear that she may be terrible, everything began to make sense.

The biggest barriers to naming our messages of the wound accurately are embarrassment, discomfort, or shame. Naming our messages of the wound requires some brave vulnerability. This is tricky, because protecting ourselves from embarrassment or exposure is often the very thing our childhood messages of the wound are designed to do. But when you courageously put words to your fears, you begin to disarm their ability to create further havoc in your adult life.

| YOU | | |
| --- | --- | --- |
| Negative Inputs | Negative Beliefs | Negative Consequences |
| (from your childhood environment, individuals, and events) | (about yourself, the world, and your place in it) | (how you function in life and in your relationships) |
| | | |

If you get stuck here, don't sweat it—but don't give up. This is hard stuff. Employ the help of safe people who know you well. I'm a fan of tapping into licensed counselors for this type of work. If you don't feel that's the best first step in your situation, then perhaps you have a mentor, a wise friend, a discerning relative, or an insightful pastor who'd be willing to listen to your story and help you spot those messages of the wound. In either case, you can do it! And I promise it will make all the difference in your life.

As you complete your chart and gain clarity on the negative consequences affecting your life today, you might find yourself feeling heavy. Before you go too far down that path, may I offer a perspective you might find helpful?

## FAULT VERSUS RESPONSIBILITY

As you look over your negative inputs column, spend some time getting in touch with how you feel about what you've discovered.

What emotions are you experiencing? For many of us, when we review the negative inputs that happened to us as kids, we reflexively (and often subconsciously) feel twinges of shame, just like we felt when those inputs happened to us decades ago. That's a problem! No child deserves the negative inputs they experienced.

It's impossible for kids to separate themselves emotionally from the harm inflicted on them by others. When bad things happen to us as children, we don't have the maturity or capacity to process those events from a rational, logical perspective. Instead, we try to make sense of it all. And the easiest way to make sense of it is to internalize the blame and create a story that leaves us responsible for things that were not our fault.

If a parent beat us or verbally abused us when we were young, we didn't have the ego strength to say, "What's wrong with Mom?" or "What's Dad's problem?" Instead, we make sense of our plight by concocting a story to explain our experience to ourselves:

- "I deserve this."
- "Mom yells at me all the time because I am bad."
- "I made Dad so mad he had to hit me."
- "I am a disappointment."
- "It's my fault my parents got divorced."

Sadly, too often we didn't invent these stories out of thin air. Our parents actually said these things to us to ease their own consciences. This makes the untruths all the more powerful and hard to get rid of. They're the very stories that become our messages of the wound, contributing to our emotional and relational pain as adults.

Most of us enter adulthood with some residual shame that was instilled in us in our formative years. We often fully believe we were responsible for what happened to us when we were kids. We believe (consciously or subconsciously) our negative inputs were our fault.

But this is the opposite of the truth!

No child *ever* deserves to be abused, mistreated, touched in the wrong way, shamed, discarded, embarrassed, discounted, overly pressured, neglected, left unprotected, or ignored. No child causes a divorce. No child causes the pain inflicted on him or her. Never. Never. *Never!* What happened to you as a child was not your fault. You are not responsible for the painful inputs that happened to you. *Hold on to that truth!*

Now that we've established this truth, let's go back and review your negative consequences column. What emotions do you feel as you study this list? It makes you uncomfortable, no doubt. Whenever I look at the negative ways my behavior has affected those I care about, I squirm. It's natural to try to separate ourselves subconsciously from the painful reality of our destructive consequences in our relationships today. We minimize or make excuses for our negative consequences. We say things like:

- "That's not my problem. It's your problem."
- "I can't help it. All the men in our family drink."
- "All the women in our family marry rotten men."
- "I'm a Johnson, and all Johnsons work hard and play hard."
- "I'm a redhead. Of course I have a temper!"
- "This is just the way I am."
- "I am *not* codependent! I'm just trying to keep my family out of the ditch."
- "I'm not controlling, but if I don't step in, she'll end up getting expelled from school."

Minimizing our responsibility for the consequence side of the equation is a problem. It's neither truthful nor helpful. Even though the negative *inputs* that left us at risk for broken behaviors in our relationships were not our fault, we alone are responsible for our negative *consequences*.

By way of analogy, let's pretend I'm sitting on my back patio while I'm writing this chapter, and a scary-looking stranger wielding a golf club runs into my backyard and approaches menacingly. He takes a swing with the club, bringing it down on my left wrist. Then he turns and runs away, yelling anti-Scott slogans as he goes.

*Well, that was weird,* I might think. I notice the force of the blow has broken my wrist. My hand dangles limply and is angled a little too far east to indicate anything short of a bad break.

There I sit on my back patio with a broken wrist, incredulous. *I didn't deserve this! I did nothing to this person to warrant this wound from him, and yet here I am with a broken wrist.* So I do what any normal person would do: I head to the ER, where they x-ray my wrist and set it in a cast. (In real life, I would also call the police. But this is a made-up story for the purpose of analogy. Work with me!)

A protective fiberglass cast makes sense, because immediately after being hurt, the best thing to do for an injury is to protect it from re-injury and minimize the damage during the critical, early time of healing. The cast is designed to keep the wrist shielded from further injury and protect the break as it heals over the coming weeks. The amount of time a fracture needs the protection of a cast is directly proportional to the severity of the injury.

But no matter how bad the injury is, at some point—whether it be four weeks or fourteen—the cast is meant to come off. After the cast comes off, is the healing done? No. What's next? Rehab. Physical therapy.

Is there anything worse than rehab? No offense to physical therapists who, in my experience, are brilliant and skilled clinicians. But going through physical therapy is expensive, painful, and time consuming. In this made-up analogy, physical therapy would be even more of a pain because I didn't deserve this injury to begin with! The harm inflicted on me was not my fault.

So let's assume that enough weeks have gone by and it's time for the cast to come off, because it's no longer needed to protect my wrist. I drive back to the doctor to have the cast removed and get my prescription for physical therapy. I feel understandably resentful. *Why should I have to do all this extra work to heal my wrist? Why should I have to endure the pain and suffering of rehab? This injury was not my fault! That stranger is the one who made the decision to hit me with a golf club. Why do I have to pay for his bad decision?*

But whether or not I deserved my injury, I am the only one who can rehab my wrist. I can't tip the physical therapist extra to strengthen my wrist for me. Even if the golf club–wielding stranger comes knocking on my door to apologize—even if he's really, really sorry that he hurt me and genuinely wants to make amends—he cannot rehab my wrist. *I am the only one who can do the hard work of healing from my injury.*

But imagine, when I get to the doctor's office I refuse to let her take off the cast. "My wrist feels just fine in this cast," I tell her. "I've decided to keep my wound safely within the comfort and protection of the cast. Wearing a cast isn't so bad. I'm used to it. I've adjusted my life around living with this cumbersome cast. Let's just leave it on."

**Question:** If I go that route, what will happen?
**Answer:** Both my wrist and I will get worse!
Eventually, much worse.

If I leave my wrist in the cast indefinitely, my skin will get gross, itchy, and smelly. Skin infections might set in. And worse than that, the wrist joint itself will soon begin to atrophy and grow weaker. I'll run the risk of neuropathy (nerve problems), and eventually I'll lose the function of my wrist altogether. In that case, who would be paying the cost of the reckless club-swinging man's behavior? Me! And frankly, not just me. My spouse, kids, and grandkids would all be adversely affected by my having a useless wrist. All because I allowed the original injury (not my fault) to cause further harm (my responsibility).

This is the bind we all face. As you look over your list of negative inputs (your version of being hit in the wrist with a golf club), you are right to feel hurt and frustrated. You did not deserve that pain. Those injuries were not your fault.

Now look over your list of the negative consequences you're experiencing today. These unhelpful patterns in your life and relationships are the equivalent of your wrist needing rehab. If you're tempted to keep your cast on long beyond its necessity, you're shirking responsibility for those consequences. How you got here wasn't your fault, but refusing to take responsibility for your own healing causes further harm to you and those you love.

It doesn't always feel fair or right, but you are ultimately responsible for your negative consequences and behaviors. Only you can rehab your wrist. Only you can heal your wound.

When you embark on healing your wounds and taking responsibility for your healing, don't do it alone. In the broken-wrist analogy, I didn't go it alone. I had a doctor, a physical therapist, an x-ray tech, a nurse, and my family to help me heal. Similarly, as you look over your list of negative consequences, remember that you shouldn't be alone on the healing journey. Find others to walk alongside you: family, friends, therapists, members of a twelve-step group, support groups, pastors, and so on. Ahead of you lies a world of hope in which you can heal from the negative parts of your story and develop new, healthier patterns of relating.

## For Reflection

Spend some time reflecting on the questions below by journaling your responses. Then, if you are comfortable, share your observations with someone who is safe and trustworthy (a close friend, a therapist, or a significant other).

- Are there any negative inputs in your story that are secrets or particularly difficult for you to think about or discuss?
- What are the distorted beliefs (messages of the wound) in how you see yourself, the world, and your place in it?
- How do your messages of the wound connect to the negative consequences and relational patterns that currently affect your life?
- What negative inputs in your story have left you feeling shame or a sense of guilt?
- In what relationships might you need to rehab your own injury by taking responsibility for the negative consequences that have adversely impacted others?

## SIX

# Automatic Responses: Taming the Reactions from Your Past

The amygdala's job is to keep us alive, and it has the neural authority to veto happiness and well-being for the sake of survival.

—Louis Cozolino, *Why Therapy Works*

James is an executive with a large manufacturing firm. He is good at his job but prone to being defensive and lashing out whenever he's criticized. He knows he has a problem and has tried to deal with it by going to counseling, working out regularly, and experimenting with deep breathing and the mindfulness exercises his therapist recommended—all to no avail. He coaches himself with internal statements to prep for meetings: "If someone doesn't agree with me, I can just listen. I don't have to get defensive." But despite his preparations, James still explodes when someone crosses him in front of those he leads. Afterward, he's filled with regret. *Why does this keep happening to me?* he wonders. *Why can't I control my reactions?*

Mario loves his job at a marketing agency and has a natural talent for the industry. He wants greater responsibility and to move upward in the company. He knows he's well-liked and successful in his current role, and everyone he knows thinks of him as a great guy. Despite this, his career has stalled for the last several years, and he doesn't really have any idea what's holding him back. But when things at work—or in his relationships— become stressful or risky, Mario withdraws. "Whenever I face a work challenge, I feel nervous or even afraid," he admits. "I go from being outgoing and confident to being timid and quiet."

Through mentoring and coaching from his supervisor and a therapist, Mario recognizes this pattern in himself and wants to change. "But whenever I sense a risk of failure, rejection, or embarrassment, I reflexively withdraw," he says. Afterward, he feels weak and sad about his inability to take the legitimate risks that would have helped him move forward in his vocation and relationships.

Both James and Mario struggle with the impact of their automatic responses, their immediate and unconscious reactions when they experience a trigger. For James, the trigger is criticism. For Mario, it is risk.

James and Mario are far from alone in their struggles. You and I experience emotional triggers as well. And we struggle to break free from responding in unhelpful ways. Despite our best efforts to respond rationally and appropriately when triggered, we often experience automatic responses, just like James and Mario.

Perhaps you can relate to some of the following scenarios:

- You are determined to speak boldly in a hard conversation but freeze up when the moment comes.
- You work hard to master a better way to react in triggering situations, but in the heat of the moment you forget everything you learned.
- You are surprised by how you overreact in certain situations.
- You kick yourself for failing to stand up for what you believe.

These are all examples of automatic responses. On the journey to telling new stories with our lives, we must learn to spot the things that trigger us and prevent them from adversely impacting our relational worlds.

## WHAT IS AN AUTOMATIC RESPONSE?

An automatic response is a natural, involuntary process in which, in an effort to protect us, the primitive part of our brain takes charge of the relational part.

When the primitive, emotional part of our brain senses danger, it takes over in order to shield us from harm. It does that by prompting us to react in ways that protect us. While this may help us feel safer in the moment, the automatic response behavior almost always makes our situations and relationships worse.

There is nothing we can do to eliminate our automatic responses completely, and we shouldn't try to. Automatic responses can save our lives when we face truly life-threatening situations. The next time you're chased by a bear, you'll be able to thank your automatic responses for the burst of adrenaline that enables you to sprint to safety.

But when it comes to relationships, automatic responses tend to muck things up. When we're triggered, we feel unsafe. And when we feel unsafe, we often react in ways that harm our relationships. The good news is that, with insight about why we react to certain situations the way we do, we can minimize the frequency and intensity of our automatic responses.

The work we've done thus far will help us in this regard. But to truly understand our automatic responses, we need to understand a few things about basic brain anatomy.

## THIS IS YOUR BRAIN

More than seventy-five years ago, Paul MacLean, a renowned physician and researcher, introduced the concept of the *triune brain*, suggesting that our brains are constructed in three concentric layers, like layers of an onion. The innermost layer, the *brain stem*, is the most primitive. The outermost layer, the *neocortex* ("new brain"), is the most advanced. And the middle layer, the *limbic system*, is where the bulk of the automatic-response actions take place.

Let's take a brief look at these three layers of the brain so we can better understand how they affect our behavior in relationships.[1]

### Brain Stem: The Innermost Layer

The brain stem concerns itself primarily with the maintenance tasks of our bodies. You can thank your functioning brain stem for the fact that, while reading this, you don't need to concentrate on staying upright, keeping your heart beating, blinking, breathing, and maintaining an appropriate blood pressure. Your brain stem is also a conduit for some of the fight-or-flight messages from your middle brain to the rest of your body.

## Limbic System: The Middle Layer

The limbic system is responsible for our emotional behavior and the initiation of our fight-or-flight response. Psychiatrist Mark Goulston described this layer as "our inner drama queen."[2]

Neuroanatomists have identified dozens of structures that reside within the depths of the middle layer of our brain. For our purposes, we'll focus on just two: the hippocampus and the amygdala.

The *hippocampus* part of the brain gets its name from the Greek word for *seahorse*, which it resembles in shape. One important function of the hippocampus relates to memory formation. The hippocampus takes in factual, objective, declarative memories and helps you store them. The hippocampus isn't the storage *location* of your memories but rather the storage *system* for those memories. So if I were to surgically remove your hippocampi (you have two, one on each side of your brain), you would still be able to recall the memories you've already stored, but you wouldn't be able to process any new memories. This area of the brain is affected significantly by the ravages of Alzheimer's disease, which is why a person with Alzheimer's might struggle to remember where they left their keys (short-term memory) but can still remember the names of the kids in their second-grade class (long-term memory).

The *amygdala*, the second important structure within the

brain's limbic system, gets its name from a Greek word that captures the structure's almond shape. It is the big actor within the middle layer of the brain.

The amygdala, like the hippocampus, plays a role in the intake and storage of memories, but whereas the hippocampus takes in factual data, the amygdala is responsible for emotional data, those memories associated with emotional intensity. As neuroscientist Joseph LeDoux observed, "The hippocampus is crucial in recognizing a face as that of your cousin. But it is the amygdala that adds that you don't really like her."[3]

The process of cataloging emotionally charged memories has a profound impact on our relationships and is a primary means by which some of our negative inputs turn into negative relational consequences. It's no surprise that the parts of the brain responsible for memory are centered in the emotional brain.

The amygdala also plays a significant role in emotional reactivity. Whenever we experience a strong emotional reaction, particularly one related to fear, our body's response and the resulting chemical cascade of fight-or-flight symptoms (rapid breathing, increased heart rate, hypervigilance, etc.) are initiated and perpetuated by the amygdala. To accomplish this protective function, the amygdalae (we have two of these as well, also on each side of the brain) are constantly watching out for danger. This primitive area of the brain is a vigilant—often hypervigilant—sentry, always on the lookout for potential danger.

These two amygdaloid functions—cataloging emotional memories and initiating protective functions—work in concert to precipitate our strong reactions to some emotional triggers. As marriage expert Brent Atkinson noted:

The amygdala draws on history of emotional conditioning and relies on gross generalization in making decisions about whether or not to trigger an emotional response. Its method is "quick and dirty," and its generalizations are "sloppy." The emotional state triggered by the amygdala may be exactly the same, regardless of whether it is a spouse who is angry with you or your father, who abused you in years gone by.[4]

In other words, your amygdala stores the emotional memories of the events in your childhood that leave you prone to (over)react emotionally when you experience a similar event today. That event triggers you into reacting to the event with emotions that may be decades old.

## Neocortex: The Outer Layer

The neocortex is the thin, outermost layer of the brain. At only two to four millimeters thick, the neocortex is the most advanced part of the brain. It is responsible for our rational and higher-level functioning: cognition (such as math, logic, and strategy) and creativity (the ability to write a poem, play an instrument, and design a building). More important for our purposes, a functioning neocortex is required for higher social functions such as forgiveness, compromise, cooperation, collaboration, empathy, sympathy, and harmony. It plays a vital role in our relationships, which is why I refer to the neocortex as the relational brain.

Now that we have some understanding of the brain's anatomy and how each part of the brain affects us relationally, let's explore how the different parts of the brain interact with each other, particularly when we experience emotional or relational stress.

## WE ARE OF TWO MINDS

To better understand how our brains create the automatic responses that impact our relationships, we're going to simplify things a little. We'll combine the first two layers of MacLean's triune model—the brain stem and the limbic system—and refer to them as a unit called the *primitive* brain. And we'll refer to the outer layer—the neocortex—as the *relational* brain. See the illustration below:

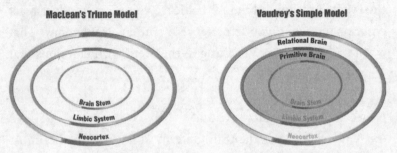

The primitive brain is focused primarily on the task of protecting us. In fact, on its own, the primitive brain really doesn't care about relationships. Its only job is to keep us safe. Therefore, in order to have fulfilling relationships and to thrive in social environments, we need an intact and functioning *relational* brain. Here's how the two parts of our brains work together.

### The Two Brains in Relationships

The table on the next page captures an important distinction between the primitive brain and the relational brain when it comes to automatic responses in relationships. If asked to guess which brain is the most accurate and precise, most of us would correctly guess the relational brain. But that precision comes at a cost: speed.

|  | Primitive Brain | Relational Brain |
|---|---|---|
| Precision |  | ✓ |
| Speed | ✓ |  |

The time it takes for the primitive brain to react to a potential threat is measured in milliseconds (thousandths of a second). In contrast, the relational brain takes much longer. Its speed is measured in tenths of a second. Thus, when the relational brain is responding to data, its interpretation is more accurate but a bit delayed; whereas when the primitive brain is responding to the same data, it responds at lightning speed, but it may be a little fuzzy on what's actually going on.

This distinction is important. Because of the speed of the primitive brain, when we're confronted by a stimulus interpreted as threatening, such as an angry facial expression or tone of voice, the primitive brain sets off a fight-or-flight cascade of neuro-chemicals and electrical responses before the relational brain has even noticed or registered the perceived risk. In other words, before we are consciously aware of the potential threat, the primitive brain has already put our body on high alert.

The two brains share a division of labor. The primitive brain quickly manages protective responses, and the relational brain accurately manages social interactions. Fortunately, in most circumstances, both parts of the brain stay in their lane and function back and forth in productive and efficient ways. We rely on the strengths of each brain for the betterment of both our safety and our relationships.

Advances in brain imaging over the last three decades, particularly functional magnetic resonance imaging (fMRI), have taught us much about which parts of the brain are active during specific situations. Researchers have discovered that the activity within our two brains is somewhat inversely proportional. In other words, when one brain is more active, the other is correspondingly less active. Imagine each brain on either side of a seesaw or a scale.

When the relational brain's activity is highest, the primitive brain's activity is lowest, and vice versa. In moments that lack emotion, such as filling out a form, the cognitive or rational part of the relational brain is the most active, and our primitive brain is a secondary player.

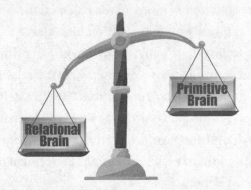

Now imagine the form you have to fill out is your tax return, and you realize you owe $6,000 in taxes. Suddenly, your protective primitive brain engages and becomes the more active brain.

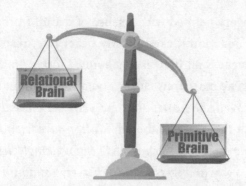

Whenever we encounter a stimulus, the input is immediately dispatched to both our primitive and relational brains. Because of their speed differences, the stimulus reaches the primitive brain first, specifically the amygdala. The primitive brain isn't precise, but it is cautious and vigilant. It quickly assesses the situation for danger. If any potential threat is detected, the primitive brain initiates a cautionary response. Remember, the primitive brain doesn't care about relationships; it just wants to protect us. So, depending on our history, it often prepares for the worst-case scenario. The good news is that most of the time, the relational brain tempers the primitive brain's overprotection by providing a more accurate assessment, exerting some executive function, and de-escalating the response.

Here's a personal example that demonstrates how this plays out in real life.

Some time ago I was scheduled to teach an evening workshop at a weekend retreat that was held on a large campus. Getting from my room to the venue required a long walk that passed through a few other buildings. About halfway there, I passed through a vast, dark room. The room appeared empty when I entered, but as I got closer to the middle, I noticed a man walking toward me holding something in his hand. At that moment I had this clear sense: *That guy has a gun!*

I was overwhelmed with a sense of dread. Immediately, my body's fear reaction kicked in. My heart rate, respiratory rate, and attentiveness all increased. *Should I tackle him? Scream for help? Run?* The man drew closer, and as I was about to pass him, I thought, *Well, he hasn't shot me yet, so I guess I'll just keep walking.* But then I remembered, *Wait, I have friends back there where he's now heading. I can't just keep walking! That's it. I need to tackle this guy and wrestle the gun away from him.*

Fortunately for me—and for the unsuspecting man—before I executed my well-intentioned but misguided strategy, I received another strong sense: *Hold on! That's not a gun. It's a wrench!* And I let the innocent man, a maintenance worker, continue on his way without harm or injury (to either of us). I didn't miss a step on my walk. By the time I exited the dark room, my vital signs had returned to normal, and I was back to looking over my notes for my talk. All this happened in just a few seconds.

So what really happened?

In this situation, the entire interplay between my protective primitive brain and my prosocial relational brain occurred as it should in an ideal world. I noticed a potential threat, but before I could overreact, my rational thinking kicked in, and I de-escalated before tackling the unwitting maintenance worker.

Part of the reason this happened as it should was because I don't have much experience with gun-packing men. My amygdala isn't preconditioned by emotionally charged memories of a violent man carrying a gun. In this setting, my primitive brain was appropriately vigilant (as opposed to hypervigilant). As a result, my response to this potential threat was a moderate code yellow: I experienced temporary fear associated with planning to protect myself and my friends until my relational brain assessed the situation with more precision and overrode my primitive brain.

But imagine how things might have happened differently if I did have emotionally charged memories about violent men or guns. I might have responded with a code-red reaction and immediately tackled the man. Remember, the amygdala's role is to take in and manage emotional memory. It plays a significant role here. The primitive brain's hypervigilance is based on past experiences, previously catalogued emotional memories. The primitive brain is hypervigilant about watching out for threats based on past experiences. It's the primitive brain that turns wrenches into guns.

Our personal history with emotionally charged memories leaves each of us with a primitive brain that is primed to be hypervigilant and overprotective in situations similar to our negative past experiences. It is in these areas that we are at greatest risk for turning a wrench into a gun and overreacting in relational settings.

In these situations, a seemingly minor emotional stimulus can trigger the primitive brain before the relational brain is even aware such a stimulus exists. The relational brain has to play catch-up in order to exert a rational, executive function and help us have a more accurate and precise understanding of reality.

The normal back-and-forth activity on the scale between the primitive brain and the relational brain is most important during emotionally charged episodes. Neurosurgical research and more recent fMRI studies demonstrate that when our emotional reaction is at its strongest, the primitive brain actually overrides the relational brain. When the primitive amygdala overreacts to a trigger related to past emotional memories, the much-needed rational perspective of the relational brain remains in the dark, leaving us without any executive function or influence. When this occurs, we experience what therapists and researchers often refer to as a *limbic hijack*, sometimes more specifically dubbed an *amygdala hijack*.

## Limbic Hijack

A hijack is a forced and unexpected theft of possession and control, which is precisely what happens when the primitive brain overrides the relational brain. It takes possession and control of executive function.

Here are some of the key characteristics of our thoughts and behaviors during a limbic hijack:

- Overly vigilant
- Lacking empathy or compassion
- Irrational thoughts
- Lacking awareness or insight
- Paranoia
- Imprecise interpretation of incoming data
- Overconfidence in interpretations

It's easy to understand the first four characteristics on this list. We might predict these characteristics, given that the rational, relational neocortex is temporarily offline. It's the last three characteristics—paranoia, imperfect data, and overconfidence— that require additional attention when it comes to relationships.

When we engage a relational situation with our primitive brains at the steering wheel, we lose the much-needed precision of the relational brain to accurately interpret what's really going on. Our only version of the story is the imprecise version told by a part of our brain that is paranoid and overconfident. One of my all-time favorite neuroscientists, Louis Cozolino, put it this way:

> When fear evokes the amygdala's primitive executive powers, anticipatory anxiety moves toward catastrophic thinking and turns worst-case scenarios into the most likely outcome.[5]

Remember, the limbic system—part of the primitive brain—doesn't care about relationships. It only wants to protect us. And the cascade of neurochemicals released when we're triggered by a perceived threat creates an exaggerated sense of confidence and decisiveness. While this cascade might help us escape when we're being chased by a bear, it doesn't help us with relationships.

Pay attention to this reality: the next time you are in a significant argument and begin to feel confident, indignant, or quite sure of yourself, it's very likely you're experiencing a limbic hijack and have actually lost the day.

When we are in a state of limbic hijack, not only do we lose the ability to be rational, we lose the ability to realize we're being irrational. *When the primitive brain interprets a situation without rational input from the relational brain, we're never more at risk for being wrong—and never more confident that we're right.* It's a recipe for relational disaster. The communication process and our capacity for relational repair falls apart.

Neuroscientists Andrew Newberg and Mark Robert Waldman described the impact of emotional charge on the relational brain this way:

> Anger interrupts the functioning of your frontal lobes. Not only do you lose the ability to be rational, you lose the

awareness that you're acting in an irrational way. When your frontal lobes shut down, it's impossible to listen to the other person, let alone feel empathy or compassion. Instead, you are likely to feel self-justified and self-righteous, and when that happens the communication process falls apart.[6]

When limbic hijack is active, we demonstrate the following:

- An overly vigilant and somewhat paranoid assessment of risk and danger
- An exaggerated reaction based on the wounds from our past
- A strong and often misguided confidence that our assessments of reality are correct

Let's revisit my encounter with the unwitting maintenance man in the dark room. Imagine that, in my past, I had emotionally charged memories related to violent men with guns. Perhaps I did a tour in a war zone or was victimized by criminal violence when I was younger. Those memories would have put me on high alert in this scenario. My primitive brain would be not just vigilant against such a perceived threat but hypervigilant about the apparent danger. The mere possibility of a gun might initiate a decisive code-red response rather than a moderate code-yellow response.

We've all experienced episodes that resulted in our amygdala storing emotional memories. As a result, our amygdalae are hypervigilant and watchful for potential danger in those areas. We're on alert (and paranoid) about those issues, and so we sometimes turn wrenches into guns.

Are you curious about the areas where you might be prone to overreaction or hypervigilance? For clues about experiences that may have primed your primitive brain to be paranoid and overprotective, review the negative inputs on the charts you completed back in chapter 5.

My primitive brain has logged plenty of emotional memories over the years. Experiences of being dismissed, devalued, and betrayed have marked my primitive brain and made me hypersensitive to any interactions that can be even remotely related to these painful experiences. (Goodbye wrench, hello gun.) Before I learned about the connection between the primitive and relational brains and my own hypervigilance triggers, this was a real problem in my relationships, particularly in my marriage. Here's a scenario that accurately represents many of the exchanges that plagued September and me in the earlier years of our marriage.

Imagine that a couple of weeks ago September and I had designated tonight as a date night. We hadn't yet planned the details, but we had agreed to go out and have dinner or see a movie. Midafternoon, I get a call from September that goes something like this: "Scott, guess what? Brenda from my small group just messaged the group and said her boss just gave her five tickets to *Phantom of the Opera* for tonight! Row D! Evidently, his family was planning to go, but they had an emergency. She's invited our entire group! I get to see *Phantom* tonight for free! Can you believe it?!"

She's completely forgotten that tonight was our date night.

Now, if I didn't possess a primitive brain or an amygdala, here's the inner monologue I would have with my relational brain: "Wow, *Phantom*! She's so excited. No wonder she forgot all about us going out tonight. That makes sense. I mean, we didn't have specific plans, and it's been a couple of weeks since we even talked about it. This actually works out fine for me. I'm an introvert and would love the chance to stay home tonight and read. September's an extrovert who loves theater. She'll have a blast seeing *Phantom* for free and socializing with her friends. This is a win-win for us both."

After that inner monologue, I would undoubtedly respond sweetly to September with something like, "Oh, honey bun! That's fantastic! I'm *so* happy for you. Have a great time." Then harps would play, birds would sing, and we'd have a beautiful, relationship-strengthening exchange. Later, when it occurs to her that tonight was supposed to have been our date night, I'll be the happy recipient of her apologies and efforts to make up.

Here's the problem: I have a primitive brain and an amygdala. In fact, I have a large, easily triggered, overactive amygdala when it comes to being dismissed or forgotten. Therefore, here's the internal monologue I'd more likely have with my primitive brain: "Here we go again! It's happening all over. Your wife is devaluing you. As soon as she has a better offer, date night is out the window. You are clearly not a priority to her. She values her friends more than you. This is unacceptable. In fact, it's an outrage! Poor you."

My past experiences at being devalued or dismissed would have triggered a limbic hijack, making me hypervigilant and paranoid. Before my relational brain has a chance to chime in and save me from overreacting, I might say something like, "So the first chance you get to ditch our date night, I'm just left in the dust? That's terrific. I see how I rate!" And we would be off to the races.

Fortunately, I am older and (a little) wiser now. I am much less likely to be hijacked by my limbic system in a scenario such as this. But let's be clear: my emotional memories are not gone. My amygdala is still paranoid and overreacts to anything remotely resembling betrayal or dismissal. But now I have insight about my risk for a limbic hijack when I'm triggered by past experiences, and that insight has dramatically increased my ability to de-escalate my primitive brain before a total limbic hijack causes harm to a relationship.

## Five Steps to Preventing a Full-On Limbic Hijack

When it comes to limbic hijacks, we face two realities. First, we all possess emotional memories that have conditioned our primitive brains to overreact in certain circumstances; therefore, we're all at risk of hypervigilant automatic responses to a spouse, a loved one, a coworker, a neighbor, a friend, and so on. (We're all at risk of turning wrenches into guns.) Second, when our primitive brains take over completely during a limbic hijack, our relational brains go offline; therefore, we're unable to have any sort of helpful dialogue until we settle down and de-escalate.

So how do you prevent a full-on limbic hijack when you're triggered? Here are five tasks that can help:

1. *Identify potential triggers in advance:* Just as James knew criticism was a trigger and Mario knew risk was a trigger, you can identify and be aware of situations that are likely to trigger your overprotective primitive brain. What types of situations leave you feeling hypervigilant about protecting yourself? Is it the risk of rejection, losing control, being sexually harassed, being publicly embarrassed, feeling inadequate, being alone, being in financial need, or being incompetent? For me, it's the risk of being dismissed or betrayed. Identifying your areas of

hypervigilance gives you the self-awareness you need to prepare for situations that could provoke your primitive brain into overreacting.

2. *Identify your go-to responses in advance:* What's your typical response when you're triggered? Do you get big, angry, and aggressive? Do you get small, shut down, and withdraw? Are you prone to be defensive or deceitful? Write a list of words and phrases to complete the sentence "I know I'm triggered when I . . ." We all have go-to responses when we're triggered. What are yours?

3. *Identify the early warning signs that you're feeling triggered:* In the early stages of being triggered—before you're fully hijacked—what does it feel like emotionally? What do you notice in your body? For your relational brain to have any hope of reversing an automatic response and preventing an overblown reaction that hurts the relationship, you must catch yourself early. Once you've tipped into a state of full-blown limbic hijack, it's too late for a neocortical (rational) rescue. As psychiatrist Mark Goulston noted: "If you're trying to talk facts and reason with the person who's in full limbic hijack, you're wasting your time. But intervene *before* the amygdala hits the boiling point, and the person's higher brain can stay in control."[7]

As you become more attentive to what goes on within your mind and body when you're triggered, you'll learn to recognize the emotional and physical changes that take place *before* you're hopelessly hijacked. For me, I feel a sense of dread I can't explain. I sometimes get a metallic taste in my mouth. Other people experience their early triggers in their stomachs, have discomfort in their chests, get flushed cheeks, or have shortness of breath. I know someone whose field of vision gets narrower and clearer as they become triggered.

It's not uncommon for us to be unaware of the early signs of our primitive brain taking over, because we've never really stopped to think about it. So be attentive the next time you start to feel triggered. What do you notice emotionally and physically? Once you get clear on your early signs and symptoms, it's striking how adept you can become at preventing an inappropriate and unhelpful reaction.

4. *Do a quick reality check:* When you start to feel triggered, remind yourself that your negative inputs and corresponding distortions of reality (messages of the wound) have preconditioned your primitive brain to be paranoid and hypervigilant. This will help your relational brain to rightsize reality as you begin to get triggered. For example, if my wife tells me she's going to see *Phantom of the Opera* with her friends on our date night, before my primitive brain starts whispering, "It's happening again! She's dismissing you. No one can be trusted. Everyone always abandons you," my relational brain can rightsize those whispers with a quick reality check: "Remember, this reaction you're having is about your past hurts, not about September or date night. It's not true that no one can be trusted. It's not true that everyone always abandons you. September has proven to be trustworthy. You're okay. You may not feel it, but everything is okay here."

5. *Share your insights with trusted friends:* Once you've worked through the first four tasks, share what you've discovered

with those in your inner circle. The purpose of disclosing your triggers is not to warn the people close to you to stay away from any triggering issues but to help them be sensitive to your most tender areas and to know you better.

Years ago I worked with a woman who was both a friend and a direct report. Early on we found ourselves in conflict every time I needed to offer some less-than-positive feedback related to her work performance. We developed a predictable pattern: I would offer the feedback, she would respond terribly, and I would become hurt and angry.

One day, as we were debriefing a recent flare-up, we decided to apply some of the principles of automatic responses. We recognized we were both getting triggered and responding poorly in these exchanges. She was feeling attacked and I was feeling abandoned. So we shared with each other some pieces of our story—our negative inputs and our messages of the wound. Once I knew her story (an abusive father who reacted aggressively whenever she made a mistake), I understood her primitive brain's oversensitivity to criticism. This helped me to be more prepared when initiating conversations in which she was primed to turn a wrench into a gun.

Notice I didn't stop offering constructive feedback—that would be a sign of an unhealthy working relationship. Instead, when I needed to offer some constructive evaluation, I knew to deliver it more sensitively, with reassurances built in. I started our dialogues by reassuring her that our relationship and her job were not in jeopardy. This helped to keep her primitive brain in check and gave her relational brain time to engage.

Similarly, once she understood my story, negative inputs and messages of the wound, she was able to receive my feedback more rationally. And in those moments when she felt I was harsh or off base, she could push back without triggering my fear of betrayal and abandonment.

By sharing our stories, we triggered each other less frequently and minimized our automatic responses when we were triggered. This resulted in years of a productive and mutually gratifying work partnership.

## THE TRICKY PROBLEM OF MEMORY

Have you ever circled back with someone after you had an argument, only to discover you both recall dramatically different versions of the original disagreement? The debrief might go something like this:

> **Person:** I was fine until you told me I *never* help with cleanup. I think I clean up a lot!
> **You:** I didn't say you *never* clean up.
> **Person:** But you did! You literally used the word "never."
> **You:** No . . . no. I'm not confused on what I said.
> **Person:** I know what I heard.
> **You:** I know what I said.
> **Person:** I'm not deaf!
> **You:** I'm not stupid!

And you're off to the races for round two (or twelve) of the argument.

This discrepancy in how we recall a disagreement is another example of the impact of automatic responses. Recall that the two structures of the brain we described earlier play an important role in memory:

- *Hippocampus:* takes in and stores our *objective, detailed* memory
- *Amygdala:* takes in and stores our *emotionally charged* memory

Even though these two structures are both within the limbic system, they relate to each other in a seesaw manner, similar to how our primitive and relational brains interact. Functional MRI scans of the hippocampus and amygdala show that when the hippocampus is busy dealing with objective memory storage, the amygdala is relatively inactive. Conversely, when the amygdala is busy taking in an emotionally charged memory, the hippocampus is relatively inactive.

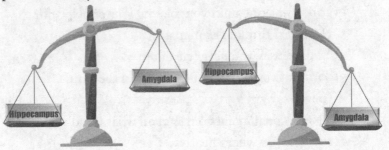

The amygdala is known for both its speed and its imprecision because it is focused on protecting you. Petty things such as detailed accuracy or protecting your relationships aren't the amygdala's concern. When we find ourselves increasingly triggered, the amygdala takes over, shuts down the more detailed hippocampus, and provides all the processing of the situation from an emotionally charged memory standpoint.

See the problem?

If you're in a situation that is calm, tension-free, and not triggering, your hippocampus is cataloging the story in an accurate, precise manner.[8] But when you're triggered, the speedy, less accurate amygdala is in charge, and the memories you process and store for later are less true to reality. Your hypervigilant, paranoid amygdala will interpret these memories with a great deal of bias.

This reality became real for me some years ago when the following exchange occurred between September and me. The memory is still vividly clear.

It was a glorious early evening in June. Our family was gathering for dinner at the beloved oval oak table we've had for more than twenty years. The large sliding glass door in our dining room was open, and the summer breeze brought with it the aromas of freshly cut grass and the chicken I had just taken off the grill. The table was set and ready. I can still see the blue plates and the wooden salad bowls our oldest son and I had brought home from a trip to Costa Rica years earlier. Everyone was seated, while I was preparing a drink at the kitchen island behind the table. My wife was seated next to my empty chair, and to her left was our youngest daughter, who was fourteen. Our sixteen-year-old son was seated to the right of my chair, facing his mother and sister. Our oldest three were off at college, so it was just the four of us that night.

That's when it happened.

My sweet wife, feeling impatient, made a comment about my making everyone wait. I felt her comment was unnecessarily critical. So, being the self-respecting man that I am, I lodged a *gentle* verbal protest, to which my wife responded by rolling her eyes.

Can you believe it?! She rolled her eyes at me! This wasn't

your typical eye roll, mind you. This was an epic eye roll that involved her whole body and was accompanied by a sneering growl.

Now, feeling completely and unfairly attacked, I lodged a more vigorous protest and then took my seat . . . to an awkward, deafening silence. Then it got even more awkward because our dinnertime rhythm was for us to join hands and pray. But I didn't dare look to my left or reach for September's hand because she was no doubt either really, really mad at me or crying. Neither scenario boded well for me.

Mercifully, my son broke the uncomfortable silence by looking at me and saying quietly, "Well, *that* seemed out of proportion."

His words and tone were kind but clear. He felt that *I* had over-reacted. *What?!* I was shocked. *Had he not seen the whole exchange?*

"I disagree," I said. "When your mom rolls her eyes at me, I feel disrespected. I was simply defending myself."

My son thought for a moment and then slowly replied, "Dad, when this all went down, you were behind me and I was sitting here facing Mom. I was looking at her the entire time." He paused and swallowed. "Dad, Mom never rolled her eyes."

Fortunately for me, by this time in my family's history, I had learned about the relationship between the hippocampus and the amygdala in the heat of battle. Otherwise, I would likely have been offended and said something like, "I know what I saw, Son. Don't try to tell me it never happened!"

But knowing what I knew, I had to pause. *Was he right?* Just in case my son was in error, I appealed to the third-base umpire, our daughter. I looked pleadingly toward her.

"Sorry, Dad," she said. "Mom didn't roll her eyes."

Now, here is an absolute truth: September's epic eye roll is still vividly clear in my memory. I can mentally replay it right now, years later, in high definition, as if it were yesterday. I am positive about what I saw, and her eye roll is still more real to me today than the laptop keyboard on which I'm typing.

*And . . . it never happened.*

When I felt criticized and a little embarrassed by September's comment about my making everyone wait at the dinner table, my hypervigilant amygdala fired an alert to protect me from experiencing a repeat of past dangers of being dismissed or abandoned. I turned a wrench (September's reasonable request that I stop dillydallying) into a gun (a demeaning eye roll in front of the kids). My primitive brain literally created a memory that never happened.

Our primitive brain is so committed to protecting us that it will prompt us into action with inaccurate, distorted, or even fabricated information, although such action will certainly strain our relationships. The lesson I learned from experience that day—and I've seen it many times throughout my vocational life—is this: when it comes to the stories we tell ourselves when triggered, our truth may not be true.

Even in the best of relationships, people still trigger each other. We're human, after all. Then what? Let's explore next how to keep our automatic responses from harming our relationships once we're triggered but not yet hijacked.

## A STRATEGY FOR DE-ESCALATION

Much has been written about de-escalation practices and strategies, and the workshop I teach on de-escalating and minimizing the impact of automatic responses requires a full day to present.

While such a detailed presentation is beyond the scope of this book, we can cover the initial and most important aspect of any de-escalation strategy.

The central point of all strategies of de-escalation can be boiled down to this one truth: when we're triggered to the point of risking limbic hijack (shown in the figure below), all efforts need to be shifted to engaging (or hooking) our rational (and fading) relational brain before it's too late. If executed early enough, this intervention can halt and reverse the progression toward hijack.

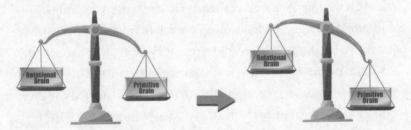

With practice, we can become aware of what's going on inside our brains and recognize the feelings associated with coming dangerously close to being hijacked. In those moments when I begin to feel triggered, I imagine tossing a life preserver to my fading relational brain to hook my desperately needed rational neocortex and pull it back into action. Doing so creates more of a balance between my primitive brain and my relational brain, which is shown in the figure below:

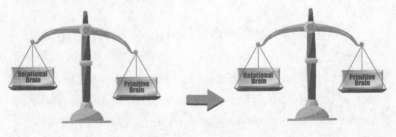

This helps ensure that I'll have a more productive conversation, because my relational brain is part of the dialogue.

Notice in the figure that we are not reengaging our relational brain to the point that we shift the balance entirely. While we want to avoid being hijacked, moving to a completely calm, purely relational brain state is not realistic or even desirable. Remember, when triggered, we are mad, scared, and/or sad. These are often appropriate emotions for the setting, and so it's wise, reasonable, and normal to let your primitive brain be attentive to what you're experiencing. In an ideal setting, when you feel triggered, your relational brain—the part of your brain that is necessary to repair a relational rift—is still contributing to the dialogue.

I'm grateful for the times when I've been able to recognize the signs and feelings that I associate with getting triggered. By recognizing those signs early on, I've been able to hook my relational brain and invite it to hang in there and contribute to the conversation. This helps me avoid misinterpreting a situation as more of a threat than it really is and prevent an automatic response that hurts the relationship. It helps me not to turn wrenches into guns.

Right about now, you might be wondering, *So how do I hook my relational brain?*

I'm so glad you asked! Here's the answer: invite it into the conversation by asking a question.

While this answer might sound straightforward, it's actually hard to do.

When my wife and I coach distressed couples on how to de-escalate during an argument, prevent a limbic hijack, and keep their relational brains in the conversation, we train them in the discipline of first sharing just the facts. (This discipline isn't only for married couples. It has dramatically improved my relationships with friends, coworkers, and family.) The most effective way to invite your relational brain to stay online when triggered is to ask, *What are the issues that all involved parties can agree on?*

For example, imagine your partner is late coming home from work. You had both agreed to a 6:00 p.m. dinnertime with the kids, and it's now 6:30 p.m. and your partner hasn't texted or called. This is becoming a recurring pattern and you are fuming. In fact, because this provokes some emotionally charged memories of your unreliable parents when you were growing up, you're getting triggered. When your partner finally walks through the door at 6:50 p.m. with no explanation for being late and no apology, you want to explode.

If you spoke your mind while triggered, the first words out of your mouth might be something like, "What's it like being the most irresponsible and selfish person who has ever walked the earth?" But you don't want to make things worse or escalate your primitive brain any further, so you quickly ask yourself, *What is a fact that both of us can agree on?*

Your first option is, "You're always late and I'm not going to stand for it anymore!" But is that a fact all parties can agree on? Nope. Your partner isn't *always* late. Finally, you land on the following: "You got home fifty minutes later than the 6:00 p.m. time we agreed on." That is a fact.

The mental process of coming up with a statement that captures the situation in a noninflammatory manner and can be agreed on by all parties will substantially de-escalate your primitive brain, because it hooks your rational relational brain into the conversation. You're still mad. You're still hurt. You may even be scared. But you are not *hijacked*. You are ready to have a mature conversation (or maybe an argument) that will have a much greater chance of resolving your relational disappointment.

The task of hooking the relational brain and pulling it back into balance is remarkably effective in all kinds of settings. Years ago, when one of our kids was worked up or a kid I was treating in the ER was frightened, I would ask them an age-appropriate math question if I sensed they were triggered and near the point of hijack, something simple, such as "Can you count backward for me from ten to zero?" The results were amazing. Intrigued by the question, they would think a moment (engage the relational brain) and then offer me an answer. After I praised them for their effort, we were then able to have a very different and more helpful exchange.

With adults, however, I stick with finding a fact-filled phrase that both parties can agree on. If I were facing a very angry September, I'm not sure I would really be able to de-escalate things if I asked her, "Hey, by the way, what's 120 divided by 4?"

I used a fact-filled phrase some time ago to de-escalate myself in a work situation. I had emailed a colleague with a quick question about a project I was working on. Our company had a policy of responding to emails within forty-eight hours, so I anticipated a prompt reply. When a couple of days had gone by without a response, I was irritated. *What's with the radio silence?*

By the third day, I began telling myself a story that my coworker was intentionally avoiding me. *Is this person mad at me? Is there some unspoken tension between us?* As I stopped to reflect on this situation, I recognized I was feeling dismissed. And this is exactly the type of situation in which I am prone to turn a wrench into a gun.

Later that day I spotted my coworker in the hallway. I

definitely felt triggered but was not yet hijacked (it was just an unanswered email, after all). As I prepared to say something, I knew I needed to lead with a fact that we could both agree on. *What should I say?*

What my primitive brain wanted to say was, "Thanks for totally blowing off my email!" But my relational brain knew better. After inviting my relational brain to help me out, I did some quick neocortical processing and landed on this fact-based statement that both my coworker and I can agree on: "I sent you an email on Monday but haven't received a response."

There, that was a factual statement with which no one involved can disagree. My coworker was able to enter the conversation with a much higher likelihood of not feeling attacked or triggered. "I got your email, but your question was beyond my area," he said. "I forwarded it to accounting to resolve. Didn't I copy you? So sorry!"

Problem solved. It was a wrench, not a gun.

Coming up with a fact-based statement that all parties can agree on hooks our relational brain to stay engaged in the conversation. This simple discipline greatly improves the trajectory and outcome of conversations that might otherwise end poorly. When you're able to get down to the facts, you're well on your way to de-escalation. More important, you avoid causing harm to the relationship.

We all experience automatic responses when triggered, but we don't have to be ruled by them. Identifying those triggers beforehand and having a method in place for when you are confronted with them puts you well on your way to building better relationships.

So what's left to learn? The robust foundation you built in

parts I and II is about to pay off. Let's turn our focus next to addressing and healing the broken parts of our stories—and begin the journey of writing new and better stories for our lives.

## For Reflection

Spend some time reflecting on the questions below by journaling your responses. Then, if you are comfortable, share your observations with someone who is safe and trustworthy (a close friend, a therapist, or a significant other).

- In what types of situations are you most at risk for feeling triggered? For example, when do you feel abandoned, imperfect, stupid, passed over, alone, smothered, in need, excluded, and so on? For ideas refer back to your negative inputs, beliefs, and consequences table (see chapter 5, page 102).
- Recall a time you overreacted and turned a wrench into a gun. What was the underlying emotionally charged memory that led to your overreaction? What emotions and physical sensations did you experience?
- Recall a recent argument you had. Generate two or three fact-based statements that all parties could have agreed on.

# PART THREE

# A NEW AND BETTER STORY

Whew! We've covered a lot of ground, and we're in the home stretch of the journey. So far you've examined your story through two lenses: the *who* of your story and the connecting threads that span multiple generations, which explain your tendencies in relationships today, and the formative inputs that led to beliefs about yourself, the world, and your place in it.

These building blocks lay the foundation you'll need going forward as you prepare to build a better life.

In this third part of our time together, we'll explore strategies for healing our wounded stories and replacing our broken plots with better ones. By the end of this section, you'll better understand:

- The three steps of healing from distorted messages (chapter 7)
- The boundaries of storytelling (chapter 8)

- A proven tool for writing your story in a way that leads to healing (chapter 9)
- The three vital characteristics that augment your healing process (chapter 10)

Depending on the depth of the wounds or distorted messages you experienced in your earlier years, the healing journey can be provocative. As you work through the concepts and exercises in this section, stay connected with the safe people in your life: friends, family, licensed counselors, mentors, pastors, and wise guides. Be kind to yourself as you go so that your journey toward a better story and a new plot will be maximally safe, productive, and healing.

## SEVEN

# Write a New Plot

If your present life story is broken or diseased, it can be made well. Or, if necessary, it can be replaced by a story that has a plot worth living.

—Daniel Taylor, *Tell Me a Story*

I can't change my tragedies, nor can I really eliminate (fully) the characters in my story, but I can write a new plot.

—Dan Allender, *To Be Told*

When I first met Amanda, a new client, I was struck by her efforts to appear fun-loving, carefree, and accommodating. She viewed herself as a great B player. "I'm just here to serve!" she said. "At home and at work, I just like to be helpful."

Helping is a beautiful thing, but something didn't ring true about how she described herself. This was an intelligent, driven woman, more eager for interpersonal growth than anyone I'd coached in recent years. Was she really just a carefree second-ary player? Was there more to her than being the B player for everyone else in her life? Time would tell.

Amanda dove into the challenge of unpacking her story.

Fast-forward three years. Today, Amanda leads an important arm of her company, parents three teens with a beautiful blend of courage and nurture, and is committed to bringing greater balance to the power differential she'd long experienced in her marriage. At her core, she still loves to help, but she has found her voice. She is now the A player in her own story.

I've never witnessed such a dramatic transformation in one per-son in such a short time. What happened to the carefree helper I met that first day? Her friends and colleagues still describe Amanda as fun, carefree, and a helper. Those are beautiful parts of her warm personality. But today, she is clear on the negative inputs she expe-rienced as a child that led to her thinking she should only ever be a background character, and she has done the hard work to rewrite her narrative. Amanda continues to inspire those around her by living out the reality that broken stories can indeed be made new and nega-tive plot points can lead to growth, healing, and better relationships.

As we dive into our journey of writing a new plot, let Amanda's story inspire you, as it does me. The relational or vocational bumps in your life don't have to be part of your future. You, like Amanda, can write a new plot. You can be the A player in your story.

## STORY REPAIR

Let's take a look at two key strategies that will help you engage and heal your story:

- Stay attentive to the root (messages of the wound).
- Travel the *awareness loop* by telling and listening to stories.

## Stay Attentive to the Root

Remember the dandelion analogy from chapter 2? Just as you have no control over the dandelion seeds that are blown onto your lawn, you had no control over the negative exposures, environments, or events that happened to you in childhood. These hurtful events were seeds that blew uninvited into your life. They then took root and grew into negative beliefs. Now you are solely responsible for the consequences or weeds that sprouted from those roots. What happened to you in childhood was not your fault, but getting the healing you need in adulthood is your responsibility. Just as it is with removing dandelions from a lawn, the most effective strategy for addressing the weeds in our lives is to attack them at the root.

We all have patterns of thought and behavior that hinder our ability to have healthy, meaningful relationships. It will take diligent effort to change those patterns. But the only way to achieve lasting success in changing old patterns is to identify and heal the distorted beliefs that lie at the root of those behaviors in the first place.

It takes quite a bit of exploration to name our distorted beliefs and then to truly understand them. That's because it's often hard to know which of our beliefs are true and which are distortions. The goal is to identify and replace the beliefs that are untrue and unhelpful distortions with beliefs that are true, helpful, and life-giving.

Retraining patterns of thought that have felt normal to you

throughout your adult life is not easy. However, it is possible if you're willing to start with the discipline of taking three explicit steps: recognize the root, refute the untruth, and revise the belief. Let's look at each one.

1. *Recognize the root:* To recognize the root means to have an accurate understanding of any untrue, unhelpful, or misguided messages you brought from childhood into adulthood. This is the most difficult part of rewriting your plot and healing your story. It requires staying open to the possibility that you may not yet fully understand your messages of the wound. So make it a practice to continually notice and isolate the unhelpful messages you are trying to repair.

   Recognizing the real wound prior to treatment is as essential to healing your story as it is to physicians in combating disease. The most serious mistake doctors make isn't in prescribing the wrong treatment to a right diagnosis; it's prescribing the right treatment to a wrong diagnosis. The same is true when it comes to your story. Stay open to the possibility of adjusting your understanding of your messages of the wound as you go, so you can apply the right treatment.

   Recognizing the root also requires noticing early on when your thoughts or behaviors are being driven by a distorted message. Again, this is difficult at first because you've been operating out of distorted messages your whole life. It's your norm. It's a bit like asking a fish to notice water. The good news is that once you've accurately named your messages of the wound, it becomes easier to spot the related, unhelpful behaviors wherever they crop up.

2. *Refute the untruth:* For some, just the awareness that messages of the wound exist—and are not true—creates enough insight to refute those beliefs. But for most of us, our responses to those long-held distortions are so reflexive and subconscious that we need additional insight, practice, and time to be able to refute them.

   As soon as we become aware that a thought or behavior is likely being spawned by a message of the wound, we must do what we can in that moment to refute the distorted belief. Whenever you catch yourself thinking or behaving according to your messages of the wound, stop and remind yourself, "That's not true!" Don't give those untrue beliefs a free pass. They have no place in your future, and the process of retraining your thinking means you need to be unflinching in giving them the boot each and every time they show up.

   Once you recognize and refute a distorted belief, you need a true and helpful message to replace it. That's where the third step comes in.

3. *Revise the belief:* Revising or replacing distorted beliefs means retraining your brain to respond in a new way when you spot thoughts or behaviors that reflect those distorted beliefs. When you see yourself going down the familiar, unproductive path, choose a different and better response.

So what does it look like in practical terms to follow this sequence? Allow me to answer that question by sharing the stories of two people I worked with, both of whom did a great job of recognizing, refuting, and revising their messages of the wound.

## Leroy: The Man Who Wanted to Meet Everyone Else's Needs

Leroy is a stockbroker who is successful in the marketplace but feels dissatisfied with his personal life. He is increasingly frustrated because he spends a great deal of his free time caring for others. Leroy is a natural caretaker, so he doesn't mind helping people he loves. But lately he's begun to resent the fact that everyone around him—his parents, his girlfriend (and the girlfriends before her), his neighbors, and even his colleagues—all seem quite happy to take more from him than they give in return. *Way* more!

**Recognize the root:** Not long after he enlisted my services as an executive coach, he shared some pieces of his story. Leroy grew up the youngest of three kids. His siblings were much older and left home when they graduated high school. Starting at age eleven, he was essentially an only child.

His mother had a severe case of lupus and was chronically ill. His father was in sales and was either on the road or relaxing in the den with the door closed. By default, much of the burden of caring for Mom fell to Leroy. The only time he remembers receiving praise or positive feedback as a child was when he was tending to his sick mother.

It took a bit of time, but as Leroy worked through his story, he gained insight into how his inputs (sick mom, absent father) led to distorted messages and consequences in his adult life; namely, he needs to be needed, and he really struggles with getting his own needs met. He has a hard time asking for and receiving what *he* wants in life. As we processed his story, he recognized two messages of the wound:

- "I am only lovable when I meet the needs of others."
- "My needs are not important."

These messages left Leroy feeling obliged to meet the needs of those around him at the expense of meeting his own legitimate needs. In fact, he felt guilty whenever someone had a need he left unmet, even when he knew meeting that particular need wasn't his responsibility. Eventually, he began to realize *he* had needs, but no one seemed interested in meeting them. The status quo worked fine for everyone else. His family, friends, and colleagues liked the old way of relating to him; that is, as long as Leroy did all the giving.

Leroy began spotting how often he reflexively reached out to meet a need and recognized that his kind gestures were often fueled by his distorted beliefs. Now it was time to refute those beliefs.

**Refute the untruth:** One early success story took place during a meeting with his boss and a peer. A call came from a client who was notorious for demanding a lot of stockbroker time but not generating much stockbroker income. Even though Leroy was much busier than his peer, the peer suggested Leroy should take the call. The boss agreed, not wanting to ruffle any feathers.

Leroy was tempted to accept the request, but then he recognized it as one of his distorted messages. *Wait a minute!* he thought. *I'm doing it again! I'm acting on the lie that I have no value in the world unless I'm meeting someone else's needs. That's not true.* This simple thought in the moment empowered Leroy to reconsider his options.

**Revise the belief:** Over time, Leroy noticed his beliefs were becoming more true and helpful. Old, now refutable beliefs were being replaced by new ones. To speed up the retraining of his thinking, he actually wrote down positive beliefs on sticky notes and put them on his bathroom mirror and on the dashboard of his car. These simple notes helped him remember what was true throughout the day:

- "My needs are important too."
- "If I choose not to meet a need, it *doesn't* mean I'm less good or less valuable."

With these revised beliefs in mind, Leroy was able to respond differently to his peer's suggestion that he should take the troubling call. "Actually, would you be willing to take the call?" he asked his peer. "My plate is full today." His peer blinked, but said, "Sure, no problem," and picked up the call.

*Wow*, Leroy thought, *that wasn't as painful as I feared*. This small win gave him confidence.

Whenever Leroy's boss or coworkers tried to pawn off unprofitable clients, he was able to say yes or no based on true, helpful messages rather than distorted beliefs. By rehearsing the revised beliefs in his head, he said no to unfair requests without feeling bad about himself. This process began rewriting the plot for Leroy.

### Barbara: The Woman Who Lived in a Dog-Eat-Dog World

Barbara is a vice president in an international tech firm. She has a reputation for being tough and demanding, but not in a good way. Several people who reported to her had quit or requested reassignment over the last year, and I was hired by her company's board as a last resort. "Barb is one of our greatest assets," her boss told me, "but she chews up subordinates faster than we can hire them."

**Recognize the root:** In our first few meetings, I learned that Barbara was born to a young mom who was fresh out of high school, and her father was unknown. Soon after she was born, her mom abandoned her newborn, skipped town, and was never heard from again. Barbara was raised by her great-aunt, a woman who was strict, distant, and demanding. To make matters worse, the only adult who seemed to care about her was a high school track coach who later attempted to exploit her sexually.

Barbara had difficulty getting a grasp on her unique messages of the wound. As she shared her story, it was clear she had never experienced safe, close relationships growing up. She learned to cope by staying isolated, self-sufficient, and aggressive. Eventually, she came to recognize her thoughts and behaviors were guided by the following distorted beliefs:

- "There is no such thing as a 'healthy relationship.'"
- "It's a dog-eat-dog world. Kindness is for the weak."

These distorted messages contributed to her feeling both alone and lonely. "I don't need anyone," she told me initially. I didn't believe her, and I don't think she believed herself. She was an intelligent and gifted woman, and she soon made the connection between her distorted beliefs and the wake she left behind at work as she drove her subordinates into the ground.

"Maybe kindness isn't only for the weak," she said, with a wry smile on her face. "And it might come in handy to have a healthy relationship or two."

**Refute the untruth:** Barbara's first win in recognizing her distorted beliefs came when a subordinate approached her with a problem. "I was between meetings," she said, "and my day was booked. I had no time for this."

Her initial reaction to the subordinate was impatience and anger. "Am I your nursemaid?" she snapped. "Do I need to hold your hand at every step?" The subordinate's face turned red and he retreated to his cubicle.

Fortunately, as a result of her newfound awareness of her messages of the wound, she caught herself, albeit too late to prevent the first damaging salvo. She told herself, *Hold it. I don't need to dominate and alienate. It's* not *a dog-eat-dog world.*

While this might sound basic to most of us, refuting her distorted beliefs with those simple phrases was a lifeline for Barbara. "After I denied the old message, I was able to reengage with the guy I blasted," she said. "I apologized for snapping and asked if the problem could hold until tomorrow when my calendar was clearer. He said it could. The whole exchange cost me only two minutes. And it would have cost just thirty seconds if I had simply responded this way in the first place. I'm learning!"

Eventually (slowly in Barb's case), the process of refuting her distorted beliefs began to retrain her brain and change how she responded to people. "I'm starting to catch myself *before* I crush the other person—*most* of the time. It's progress, and I'll take it!"

**Revise the belief:** When Barbara recognized she was acting out of the messages of the wound and refuted the distorted belief, she reminded herself of truer and more helpful beliefs:

- "Strong people can be kind. In fact, they *should* be kind!"
- "Fulfilling relationships are possible *and* desirable."

I don't want to suggest that as a result of her family-of-origins work, Barbara is now a cuddly teddy bear. She's still a formidable force at work. But I will say that she has learned to treat her peers and coworkers with respect. And in turn, her relationships with others are improving, sometimes dramatically.

"Turns out I can be both successful and kind at work," she said. "Who knew?"

## Travel the Awareness Loop

Some years ago I was driving through the Rocky Mountains, and I came across a roadside farmer's market with several booths. I pulled over to stretch my legs.

Out front, I noticed a grizzled, silver-haired, middle-aged man standing next to some giant knotted chunks of lumber and a chain saw. His booth bore the sign, Chain Saw Art. Next to the logs was a series of detailed wood carvings of local wildlife: bears, eagles, salmon, and elk. The beauty and delicate detail of the carvings were breathtaking; so exquisite, in fact, that I found it hard to believe these statues were really the result of this man and his chain saw. So I struck up a conversation.

His name was Earl and he was a third-generation chain saw carver. When he sensed my disbelief, he grinned and said, "I'm about to start a new statue right now. Why don't you just stick around and see for yourself." So I did.

"First, I decide what animal I'm gonna carve, and then I find the right log for the job," he explained. "This one's gonna be a black bear standing on its hind legs."

He wrestled a four-foot piece of tree trunk into a standing position, put on his safety goggles, and fired up his chain saw. Then he began lopping off large chunks of wood. "These pieces are hindering the final product," he hollered over the noise of the saw. He lopped off several smaller chunks, then turned off his saw and took a few paces back to survey his progress and the wood that remained. The log now showed a roughly shaped bear: head, two arms, and two legs. Very coarse.

Earl took a few moments to assess the log from all angles. Then, with a slightly smaller chain saw, he went back to work. He repeated this cycle a number of times. Cut. Evaluate. Cut. Evaluate. It was mesmerizing. I stepped away briefly to explore the rest of the farmer's market, but I could hear Earl's chain saw constantly buzzing away in the background. I stopped by a few more times to watch his progress. By the time I left, the weather-beaten log he'd started with had become an exquisite black bear. The bear was truly a work of art, carved with such detail it took my breath away. "All with chain saws," he said. "One lap at a time."

Earl's cut-and-evaluate strategy is something I recommend for all of us as we take further steps to engage our story. When we make progress recognizing, refuting, and revising our distorted beliefs, something beautiful happens: our level of self-awareness increases. This improved insight gives us a new and better vantage point to reassess our reality. Just as Earl took time to turn off his saw, step back, and survey his progress, we would be wise to do the same. Where are we? What progress have we made? What areas still need work?

We've made progress, and because we've made progress, we can move on to more detailed refinements. We can take a new and even more accurate look at ourselves, the world, and our place in it. And we repeat the process again and again.

This refinement is possible when we invite synergy between two primary activities:

- Becoming more self-aware
- Telling and listening to new stories

I call this synergy the awareness loop.

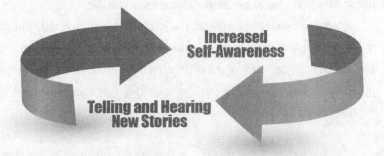

With new levels of self-awareness comes a welcome reality: you are now able to tell new and more accurate stories. And with improved self-awareness, you're better equipped to listen to the stories of others and hear them in increasingly redemptive ways, both for your own benefit and for the benefit of the storyteller. You can be present with others in their story as they tell it, and as you listen, you're better able to glean and apply insights from their stories to your own.

Theologian Frederick Buechner captured this important concept when he wrote: "My story is important not because it is mine, God knows, but because if I tell it anything like right, the chances are you will recognize that in many ways it is also yours."[1] It has been my experience that the more we listen to other people's stories, the more accurate and nuanced our understanding of our own messages of the wound become. We learn by listening.

"The best antidote to incomplete or faulty stories is more stories from different tellers," Daniel Taylor observed.[2] I couldn't agree more. In my own life and in the lives of people I've coached, I've seen firsthand the power of traveling the awareness loop. Telling and listening to stories begin a productive loop of growth and healing. As we exchange more and new stories, our self-awareness grows and perpetuates a healing cycle.

Even hard-driving Barbara, the executive who lived in a dog-eat-dog world, experienced the value of traveling the awareness loop. Remember, after examining her story, Barbara's initial assessment led her to the conclusion that her messages of the wound were:

- "There is no such thing as a 'healthy relationship.'"
- "It's a dog-eat-dog world. Kindness is for the weak."

However, in the ensuing months of our meeting together, she told and heard more stories in other settings, primarily with a neighbor and with a weekly social group for female executives. In these safe settings, she spotted a new theme. When she told her story, she noticed herself sharing how she expected she would always be alone. In contrast, as she listened to the stories of others, she noticed they told stories that suggested they fully expected to always be in relationships with others and even expected to be pursued. It made her curious.

After several cycles on the awareness loop, Barbara became aware of two more distorted beliefs she had been unable or unwilling to acknowledge. Her primary and most destructive messages of the wound were actually:

- "I will always be alone."
- "No one wants me."

These distorted beliefs were rooted in Barbara's having been physically abandoned by her mother, abused by her high school track coach, and emotionally abandoned by the great-aunt who raised her. Once she recognized these distorted beliefs as untrue, she was able to recognize, refute, and revise them with a message that was truer and more useful: "I don't have to be alone. I can be someone who is wanted by others."

When Barbara shared these new insights with me, her eyes grew moist. "I think I actually want people in my life," she said. "Maybe one day I might even want a permanent someone in my life." Once Barbara had this breakthrough, her healing and relational growth accelerated rapidly.

Story repair is a necessary but less-than-easy process to go through as we walk toward healing and better relationships. But, luckily, there are some practical tools we can use to take this step so that we not only address the distorted messages that have caused us so much trouble but also continually become more self-aware as we go, gaining further insight, making healing corrections, and experiencing even greater growth.

## For Reflection

Spend some time reflecting on the questions on the next page by journaling your responses. Then, if you are comfortable, share your observations with someone who is safe and trustworthy (a close friend, a therapist, or a significant other).

- Briefly review the inputs, beliefs (messages of the wound), and consequences you've identified previously. What progress have you experienced in refuting untruths and revising beliefs? In what ways, if any, do you feel stalled or stuck?
- What messages of the wound do you suspect might need to be reconsidered and revised? How might you refute and revise these beliefs into something truer and more useful?
- In what ways might you enlist the help of your trusted person? For example, ask them to check in when you seem to be returning to thoughts and behaviors consistent with your messages of the wound rather than your revised beliefs.

# EIGHT

# Tell Your Story

Your life is not like a story; it is a story. And if any part of it is to have significance beyond you, this story must be told.

—Daniel Taylor, *Creating a Spiritual Legacy*

Jonathan was a happy-go-lucky guy who worked hard and played hard. I hired him for a job that required emotional flexibility: celebrating with those he served one day and consoling others in seasons of pain the next. Through it all, Jonathan seemed unaffected and unfazed by either extreme. He did amazing work, with one exception: whenever he faced a client who became demanding or aggressive, he would either quickly give in to the client's excessive demands or shut down completely.

This issue came to a head after Jonathan conceded to expectations that were not only inappropriate but quite costly to our company. It was so out of character, even for his pattern of giving in, that it made me more curious about his story. I had heard bits and pieces of it over the first couple of years he worked for me, but there were gaps in my understanding, particularly around his early years and his father. With his continued employment in jeopardy, Jonathan decided to get serious about understanding his negative consequences in the context of his story. He began seeing a therapist, and he and I began to get more intentional about processing his story during our one-on-one meetings.

It was only when Jonathan began sharing further details that he (and the rest of us) understood the impact of growing up with a verbally and physically abusive father and a mother who failed to protect him. Suddenly his passivity when confronted with someone's anger made complete sense.

"Whenever someone loses their temper, I feel like I'm five years old again," he said. "I want to cry and run for cover." Jonathan now had a target on which to focus his healing work.

As a result of identifying and overcoming his distorted messages, Jonathan was able to grow in confidence and courage in those tense situations. He went on to become one of the most valuable employees I ever had. But the growth and healing Jonathan sought began only after he shared his story with others in greater depth.

Jonathan's experience is a great example of the power and purpose of sharing our stories with others. But what does it look like to tell one's story in a maximally helpful way? Often when we tell our stories to others, we inadvertently sabotage our efforts by not sharing our past with adequate breadth or depth. Let's take a deeper look at telling our stories in a way that maximizes new insights, both for ourselves and for those listening.

## BREADTH: SHARE FROM ALL FOUR QUADRANTS

To tell our stories effectively, in a way that brings healing, we need to tell the full breadth of our story. But oftentimes we struggle to do this. We tell a piece here and a piece there, but we don't see how all the pieces connect. Why is that? To understand we need to step back and look at the scope of what the human experience includes.

We are complex creatures, and there are myriad ways of understanding or categorizing the various aspects of what it means to be human. For our purposes, we'll focus on four: the physical, the emotional, the relational, and the spiritual.

| PHYSICAL | SPIRITUAL |
|---|---|
| EMOTIONAL | RELATIONAL |

The *physical* aspect is the part of our being that engages the outside world with our five senses: sight, hearing, taste, smell, and touch. We rely on our bodies to carry us around. When we twist an ankle or fall down, we get a bruise, a sprain, or even a bone fracture, and it hurts. When we get a cut, we bleed. When we get a great night's sleep, we wake up refreshed. When we eat a healthy meal and drink plenty of water, we feel good inside. We're energized. This physical component of our beings sometimes gets ill and eventually wears out and dies. Positive or negative, our physical nature affects us every day.

The *emotional* aspect includes our internal experiences, such as our thoughts, moods, intellect, and feelings. Though they cannot be seen or touched, our emotions affect us in very real ways. Our emotional experiences can be characterized by moments of happiness and excitement, as well as by moments of anger or fear. The emotional dimension is the aspect that relates to our internal world.

The *relational* aspect is the part of us that engages with other people. Everything related to love, romance, friendship, conflict, intimacy, cooperation, generosity, teamwork, and sense of justice fits into this quadrant.

The *spiritual* dimension is the aspect of our being that connects with the transcendent. This includes how we relate to God or a higher power, our understanding of good and evil, our practice of faith, and our beliefs about an afterlife. While each of us may have unique views about what comprises the spiritual realm, only the staunchest atheist would claim there is nothing beyond the material world. And even the belief that there is no spiritual dimension would fall within the spiritual quadrant.

Sometimes we struggle in one or more of these quadrants:

- *Physical:* Our bodies become ill or out of shape.
- *Emotional:* We feel sad, depressed, angry, or frightened.
- *Relational:* We are isolated, lonely, or in conflict with others.
- *Spiritual:* We find our faith is weak or feel disconnected from or even abandoned by God.

When we start having trouble within a particular quadrant, we typically respond in one of two ways: we deny the problem or we seek help.

Let's look at both of these responses in a little more detail.

## Response 1: We Deny the Problem

Sadly, denial is a common first response when we have a problem. In addition, we are often inconsistent with how attentive we are to each of the quadrants. We might be extra attentive to one quadrant at the expense of other quadrants. For example, I know a woman who is conscientious about maintaining her mood (the emotional quadrant). She reads every book on depression she can find and sees a therapist weekly. And yet her marriage (the relational quadrant) and the condition/care for her body (the physical quadrant) are in terrible disarray and go largely ignored.

Here's the kind of trouble we get into when we deny or ignore a problem in a quadrant:

- *Physical:* We disregard that we are gaining weight, becoming out of shape, or getting easily winded on the stairs. We ignore the lump, cough, or unexplained weight loss. We continue to take risks that are careless, can be dangerous, or leave us susceptible to disease and injury.
- *Emotional:* We feel ashamed of our depression, sadness, or anxiety and so avoid seeking help. We conclude that nothing will change and end up settling for a much less fulfilling life.
- *Relational:* We believe a distorted story about ourselves and others: "People are untrustworthy and selfish," "It's my job to please others," or "There is something terribly wrong with me." And we settle for a lifetime of

unsatisfying, superficial relationships, repeated conflicts, or loneliness.

- *Spiritual:* We don't feel as if we are experiencing a higher power or can't make sense of the broken state of the world that is allegedly run by a good and powerful God. We stop trying to engage or understand the parts of the world that are supernatural, unexplainable, or even miraculous. When we ignore the spiritual aspect of our lives, we may be prone to hopelessness, the world might not make sense, and life may seem without purpose.

When we deny or ignore a problem in any quadrant, we stay stuck. But when we acknowledge a problem quadrant, we at least know we need help. What now?

### Response 2: We Seek Help

The second and more productive strategy when we have a problem is to get help from others. It has been my experience that when we sense we need help, most of us tend to look for it in the following predictable sequence:

1. Google it.
2. Buy a book on the topic.
3. Talk to a safe friend or relative.
4. Talk to less safe but smarter friends.
5. Seek help from a professional.

Only when we have exhausted steps one through four do we consult a professional. If we have a problem in the physical realm, we consult a physician or a physical trainer. In our emotional and relational worlds, we seek out a therapist or life coach. And when our unsatisfied spiritual longings require professional intervention, we meet with a pastor or a spiritual guide.

This is good. However, we've probably had the experience of doing all of the above and things still didn't improve. Why?

At least part of the problem lies in the fact that we compartmentalize our problems. This presupposes we are, in fact, comprised of distinct compartments.

We are not.

The quadrant model we began with implies that the four aspects of our being are separate and independent, as if we were a house with four distinct rooms. Such sharp divisions are not accurate. We are multidimensional creatures, but our different dimensions are not separate compartments. They are interconnected, and the lines between the compartments are permeable. When one quadrant is out of whack, it affects the other three. For example, when you get sick (physical), this has an impact on your mood (emotional). If your romantic interest rejects you (relational), this impacts your feelings about God (spiritual) or how you sleep (physical).

I believe we are less like houses with several rooms and more like a bucket of paint with four colors poured and mixed inside. We cannot simply examine a single color by itself; it's part of the whole. If it's true that the four aspects are much more intimately integrated and interdependent, what are the implications?

## My Quadrant Problems

Twenty years ago, if you had asked me to give you a personal state of the union, I would have reported that things were going okay overall. However, there were a couple areas in my life I knew, deep down, were not quite right. This angst expressed itself primarily in two quadrants: the relational and the spiritual.

Relationally, I was lonely. I did not have deeper friendships. For the most part, I got along fine with people. I was attentive and affectionate with my wife and kids, and we often had friends over. However, something was not right. I felt isolated, unknown, and misunderstood.

I shared my struggles with some friends. "I'm feeling distant from people," I told them. "I'm lonely. I love you guys, but I want deeper friendships, and they seem to elude me."

My friends offered their insights.

"You're just not friendly enough. You need to smile more."

"You should read *How to Win Friends and Influence People*. It'll help you be more social."

"You should come to more of our gatherings."

"You should . . ."

So I followed their advice. I tried to be friendly. *Smile! Smile! Smile!* I disciplined myself to smile so big and so long that my face hurt.

"Good morning!" *Smile! Smile!*

"Good to see you!" *Smile! Smile!*

"Want to come over for dinner?" *Smile! Smile!*

No doubt my forced smile left people more frightened than welcomed. They probably feared I was approaching them to awkwardly overshare or possibly sell them something.

I also devoured the Dale Carnegie classic *How to Win Friends and Influence People*, which I heartily recommend. It's a great book. I soon owned this book in paperback, hardback, cassette, and the latest media rage—compact disc (it was the early nineties).

I learned valuable stuff about relating to people. My demeanor was warmer, I suppose, but I felt no less isolated. My relational problem even worsened. What was wrong?

Spiritually, I felt God was distant and disapproving. If I did connect with God through prayer or solitude, I assumed God was angry and disappointed in me. This sense of rejection was so unsettling I began to avoid any attempt at connecting with God. I continued to do the religion thing: read my Bible, attended church services faithfully, and went to my men's small group. I even read theological commentaries. But none of these helped. I remained certain I was a failure in God's eyes. I began to wonder if I was actually a spiritual fraud. Maybe I was even an atheist?

What made these struggles particularly troubling in this season (especially the atheist part) was that, at the time, I was an elder in my church. *Uh-oh.* Eventually, my spiritual distance became great enough that I mustered up the nerve to share this with a small group of Christian leaders. (This was before Google existed, so I skipped step 1.)

"I feel like God is distant and disapproving," I told them, "and it's causing me to avoid trying to connect with God. I worry that my desire for God is waning, and I feel like a hypocrite."

These friends responded in exactly the same ways I had often responded to others in this situation, which, I'm now embarrassed to admit, was with statements such as these:

- "Well, whenever there is distance between you and God, it's not God who moved."
- "Your spiritual problem probably indicates the presence of unconfessed sin in your life."

- "How often are you reading your Bible? You need to get back into the Word."
- "What does your prayer life look like? Are you praying enough?"

I believe there are times, places, and contexts in which this sort of counsel could be valid or helpful. But in my situation, it only added to my sense of shame, isolation, and desperation. I had already doubled up the time I spent praying, journaling, and reading. I was already convinced some misstep on my part must have resulted in the distance I felt.

Nonetheless, I followed my friends' advice and redoubled my efforts. And my spiritual problem only got worse. What was going on here?

A couple of years later, while working on my master's degree, I was in an environment in which it was normative (actually expected) to share our stories with one another. In addition, I met weekly with a mentor who asked to hear my story.

Up to that point, whenever someone asked me about myself, I offered up a short bio with just the basics. "My name is Scott. I'm married to September, and we have five kids."

When I offered that version this time, my mentor stopped me. "No," she said with kindness. "I want to hear your *story*."

"Why?" I asked.

"Because it's healing and redemptive for you to know your own story," she replied.

"Um . . . but I already know my own story, I was there," I said sarcastically. "But thanks for asking."

My mentor sighed, recognizing I was going to be a remedial case. Undeterred, she changed strategy. "Okay. The other reason I want you to tell your story is that I want to get to know you better. Our group wants to know you better. We can't possibly know you without hearing your story."

Feeling perturbed that she wasn't satisfied, I tried again. "Okay, I live in West Dundee, I have five kids, and—"

"No. Your *story*! Your *whole* story. Start from the very beginning. Where were you born? Tell me about your parents. Where did you live as a kid? What were you like? Tell me about your friends, your home, and its environment. What made you laugh? What made you cry? Tell the whole story."

"But that could take hours," I protested.

To which my mentor, without pause, replied, "Of course it will. I would like the first hour today, please."

So I started telling her my story, and I started at the beginning. It was harder than I thought because, up to that point, I hadn't really thought about this stuff. It seemed very touchy-feely, which made me uncomfortable. During that first hour, I told the story of my early life with the same level of emotion I would bring to filling out a tax form. No feeling, no connection. Just fact after fact.

I stared out the window of her office and droned on with a fairly colorless report of my early years. At one point, I looked over at my mentor and she had tears in her eyes. *What? What's the matter with this woman?*

"Have I said something wrong?" I asked.

"Scott, parts of your story break my heart," she said.

I was surprised and taken aback. *Yikes. My story is not that dramatic. What's her deal? I wanted a mentor and I got a weirdo!* I had come to this woman to be mentored because she was highly respected as someone who could help me become a more successful leader. I wasn't interested in excessive sentimentality or a pity party. I still had quite a bit of skepticism in this whole "tell your story" assignment. It sounded like code for "Whine about your problems, you loser!" I had no stomach for this. *Sigh.* That was week one.

I returned the next week and continued telling my story. Once again, when I looked up while describing a rough patch in my past, I saw my mentor had tears in her eyes. I was baffled and a bit exasperated.

"Okay, I'm done," I said. "What does any of this have to do with making me a better leader?"

"Scott, based on some of these stories, I fear it must be very hard for you to trust or really connect with anybody in this world—even God."

*Whoa. How did she know?* A light bulb went on.

My mentor's observation that day began a revolution of thought in me that was nothing short of clouds parting and angels singing. That one comment, "I fear it must be very hard for you to trust or connect with anybody," opened up a whole new world of understanding myself and connecting the dots between my story and the relational and spiritual struggles that had plagued me for years. What if I didn't have a *relational* or *spiritual* problem so much as an *emotional* one? What if my unidentified and unaddressed emotional wounds from the past were at the root of my struggles with people and God? Perhaps I was stuck because, all this time, I was applying relational and spiritual solutions to an emotional problem? Maybe attending to my emotional problem would actually be the best way to solve my relational and spiritual problems.

Suddenly I had hope.

# FROM COMPARTMENTALIZATION
# TO INTEGRATION

My experience demonstrates both the risk of trying to address problems in a compartmentalized manner, as well as the tremendous gain that can come by taking an integrated or wholistic approach. Up to that point, I had diagnosed my distance from God and lack of meaningful friendships as spiritual and relational problems, and thus prescribed myself a treatment to remedy those ailments: pray more, read the Bible more, and Smile! Smile! Smile! It had no positive effect because my problems were primarily emotional, even though they were expressed with spiritual and relational symptoms. I was tackling my issues as if I could isolate one quadrant of myself, lay it on a table for examination, repair it, and then put it back. But in reality, the ability to isolate one dimension for examination is about as likely as reaching into a can of green paint and pulling out some yellow.

Since that season, I've wholeheartedly embraced the importance of telling and listening to each other's stories when it comes to personal growth in all aspects of our lives. I've become much more attentive to healing the fractures within all quadrants of my life—regardless of the presenting issues—and the results have been deeply satisfying. My intimacy level with my wife and kids has made dramatic improvements. I've built a small network of deep, lifelong friends. And I have a sense of God's tender presence and unconditional love for me that, as I type this, leaves a lump in my throat.

My experience is unique because of the high-quality mentor who helped me process my story (yes, she was amazing). Not everyone has access to the level of discernment, experience, and wisdom I did during the initial seasons of learning to tell my story. I was fortunate indeed. However, the mentoring was not the only catalyst for the narrative repair I experienced.

During the entire season I was meeting with my mentor, I was also part of a small cohort of fellow grad students who met weekly. The first time I told my story to this group, after weeks with my mentor, they seemed overly moved and concerned about some of the elements of my story, events that had always seemed unimportant to me. Judging by their facial expressions and by the questions they asked, I began to realize that perhaps there was room for reinterpretation when it came to how I perceived some of my early relationships and experiences. I was seeing parts of my story reflected back to me through their eyes, and what I saw surprised me.

Now, to be clear, I do not have stories of significant abuse in my past. In many ways, I had what might be considered the typical 1960s/1970s upbringing. But I—like you, like my kids, like everyone this side of heaven—experienced hurts and wounds from childhood and from parents, teachers, friends, and neighbors that left a lasting impact. While there were many bright spots in my childhood for which I'm grateful, there were also some rough spots that wounded me emotionally. Past experiences I had always tried to pass off as insignificant probably played more significant roles in my adult life than I realized, until I saw them mirrored back to me through the objective eyes of benevolent listeners. My peers weren't trained therapists or professional mentors. They were simply attentive friends. But their responses and observations were invaluable.

Similarly, one of my most impactful relationships during this season was an older friend I'll call Phil. He was an auto mechanic and unsophisticated in matters of bonding, transference, attachment disorders, codependence, narrative repair, spiritual direction, interventional prayer, or any of the other mechanisms my primary mentor was trained in. Nonetheless, Phil became a primary catalyst for my liberation. What did he do? He was present with me. He listened and gave honest feedback about how he interpreted my story and how he felt about me and our relationship. I watched his face as I told him my story. I experienced his empathy and interest on my behalf. From the questions he asked, I felt heard and advocated for. I was able to more accurately interpret my story through Phil's eyes. Equally important was the fact that Phil also shared his whole story with me. Hearing his story was another profound way that helped me to better contextualize and understand my own.

Phil was a guy willing to listen, give feedback, and advocate for me. My cohort of grad students weren't trained professionals; they were just a bunch of friends who asked questions and mirrored back what they saw. And it made all the difference. Since then, I have come to believe it should be normative for average people to come alongside average people in redemptive ways.

As you seek to do this in your own life, sharing with other people who are willing to come alongside you, use the table below to help you capture and share the full breadth of your story:

| Life Stage | Physical | Emotional | Spiritual | Relational |
|---|---|---|---|---|
| Childhood | | | | |
| Adolescence | | | | |
| Young adulthood | | | | |
| Adulthood | | | | |

The bottom line is this: tell your whole story—the long version, all four quadrants—going back to when you were a kid. Don't assume you have connected all the dots of your life by keeping them in the vacuum of your own mind, as I did for years. Don't assume you understand all the cause-and-effect relationships of your early years or which dimension houses your primary struggles today. Invite some trustworthy everyday people to come alongside you and tell them your story. And then listen to theirs. You'll all be better for it.

## DEPTH: EVEN THE HARD PARTS

When you tell someone your story, the question to ponder about depth is this: How much is too much? There are two mistakes we can make: sharing too deeply too early or sharing too lightly and avoiding the hard stuff.

When you share too deeply too early, you fail to be a good steward of your life story. The nitty-gritty details of your story shouldn't be casually tossed into any old conversation. They should be reserved for someone who is safe, willing to listen, and trustworthy, such as a close friend or a licensed counselor. It's a mistake to overshare right away with a new listener or group. Your story is a precious commodity with which you must not be reckless. Once trust and safety are established, and only then, you can let it all out.

In my experience, the mistake of oversharing by telling too much too soon is rare. Most people (myself included) err on the side of sharing too little of their stories because they have a hard time sharing to begin with. It's much more common for people to undershare.

Telling only the lite version of your childhood and past experiences, passing over the traumatic or embarrassing parts, jeopardizes the healing and growth potential of telling your full story.

Let me give you an illustration from my years in medicine, which shows the importance of sharing the painful parts of our stories. One of the most common presenting complaints in any emergency room is a skin laceration, namely, a cut. Even though lacerations aren't typically as challenging or dramatic as most other cases in a trauma center, wound repair was always one of my favorite problems to manage, because each wound was unique and presented its own challenges. And when they were stitched well, the results were tangible, visible, and immediate.

Over my years in the ER, I repaired thousands of cuts, some simple and others very complicated. I came to recognize a few predictable characteristics of laceration patients, particularly with young patients. The typical story went something like this.

A kid accidentally cuts himself and rushes, crying and bleeding, to the nearest parent. The parent then grabs a towel—usually the oldest, most mismatched towel they own—and wraps it around the injury to stop the bleeding and save the living room carpet. If both parents are home, a bartering process ensues to decide which parent must take the kid to the ER. The loser of rock paper scissors then loads the kid into the car—towel and all—and heads to the hospital.

Upon arrival, the kid is pretty terrified, though trying to put on a brave face. The accompanying parent's level of anxiety is inversely proportional to how many children he or she has; the fewer the children, the higher the anxiety. New parents tend to be more petrified than their bleeding child, whereas well-seasoned parents use the time to browse through the waiting room's maga-zine rack or scroll on their phone.

Whenever I'm tempted to minimize parts of my story, a spe-cific ER case comes to mind. The patient was a boy, about seven years old, whose home abutted a strip mall that was undergoing significant remodeling. One afternoon, this boy (we'll call him Troy) discovered, to his delight, a large stack of twelve-by-twelve-inch glass panes stacked in the paved alley for the trash pickup the next morning.

What are the odds a seven-year-old boy would discover such a treasure and leave all that beautifully stacked glass unbroken until morning? *Zilch*. Next to lighting stuff on fire, nothing amuses and excites a boy as much as breaking glass.

As you might expect, Troy got busy breaking the glass panes. He tossed the panes into the air and watched each one smash to earth with a gratifying shatter. But things soon took a frightening turn. After he had tossed five or six into the air and watched them crash, large fragments of glass covered the pavement all around him. Troy tossed another pane above his head, but as it reached its zenith and began to descend, he realized it was heading right for his upturned face! He dove out of the way, sparing himself certain facial trauma, but then he slipped and fell on the broken shards at his feet, giving himself a long, deep, jagged laceration on the underside of his left forearm.

Blood was everywhere. Troy ran home and found the nearest parent—in this case, his mother—who grabbed a Teenage Mutant Ninja Turtles towel, wrapped his arm to control the bleeding, and brought him to our emergency department. Upon arrival, Troy appeared terrified. His mom was merely annoyed that he had been playing with glass (Troy was her fourth son).

Once he was checked in, I grabbed Troy's chart and headed into his room. He sat on the gurney, eyes wide open, cradling his arm in the towel. Mom sat nearby. She set down a *People* magazine and stood to shake my hand.

I tried my usual doctor small-talk routine to help Troy relax.

**Me:** So, Troy, it says here in your chart that you're seven.
  Is that right?
**Troy:** Yes sir.
**Me:** Second grade?
**Troy:** Yep.
**Me:** Married?
**Troy:** What? Ew! No!

He smiled slightly. We chatted a bit more. But sooner or later in these cases the moment of truth comes: I needed to go for the Teenage Mutant Ninja Turtles towel to examine his wound.

"I hear you've cut your arm," I said. "Let's take a look."

As I reached for the towel, Troy did what every child does (and what every adult wants to do) in this situation: he pulled his arm away and out of my reach.

At this stage of the predictable dance, Troy's mom chimed in with the standard parent response: "Honey, if you don't let the nice doctor see your owie, he can't fix it." (Where did she get the idea I was nice?)

**Troy:** Okay! Let's go home.
**Mom:** Troy, we have to get your arm fixed. You have a bad cut!
**Troy:** I know, but not now. I'm not ready. Let's come
  back tomorrow.

And so it continued back and forth until Troy finally surrendered his injured limb. If the kid wasn't crying before, this is where the tears begin.

Usually, the surrender of the wound is preceded by an unfortunate statement from the parent: "Don't worry, honey, this isn't going to hurt a bit." This, of course, is a lie. Because the truth is, it always hurts to expose our wounds. But expose we must, because of an even more compelling truth: *we cannot heal what we do not expose.*

Even if we believe this to be true, we often behave as if it's not. At a cognitive level, Troy knew he had a problem: he had a bad cut on his arm, and it wouldn't stop bleeding. And, even at age seven, he knew the only way to get his problem solved was to give me access to his arm. He knew that if he didn't surrender his wound to my care, his arm wouldn't get better. Nevertheless, despite knowing all this, Troy vehemently resisted exposing his wound to me, the one person in the room who could help.

He tried everything he could to avoid removing the towel and exposing the real problem:

- He promised he would wear a Band-Aid and let the cut heal on its own.
- He assured me it really didn't hurt right now and he'd be fine.
- He showed me how his arm was working just fine. He bent his elbow up and down, tenderly holding the towel in place. This was his seven-year-old way of insinuating that his mother and I were both overreacting.
- He promised he would never throw glass again.

When these tactics failed, he asked for a temporary reprieve. "We can come back tomorrow," he said. "Or next week. This isn't a good time for me. I promise to be careful until then." He was a sharp kid and rather adorable in his earnest efforts.

Earlier that day, when Troy first cut his arm and was experiencing the full pain and consequences of the wound, he didn't resist coming to the doctor. He knew he needed help. He probably had every intention of doing whatever the doctor told him in order to get the problem fixed. But when the moment arrived, and I needed to actually remove the towel so healing could begin, his instinct kicked in and he resisted.

By now I bet you can see where I'm headed. Seven-year-olds with glass cuts aren't the only ones who panic when it comes time to expose their wounds. You and I use this wound-protection strategy as well. We've all experienced relational pain and wounds that have distorted how we see ourselves, the world, and our place in it. We want help. We know we need help. And yet, when it is actually time to get help, we often resist exposing these tender, wounded places to others, the hearers of our stories, the very people who could help with our healing.

In an effort to appear open to help, we may offer other aspects of our story. We say we are an open book (except for *that* story, we say to ourselves). Unfortunately, this strategy doesn't cut it. It's the equivalent of Troy willingly inviting me to examine his other arm and either or both of his legs.

Too many of us choose to stay a hostage to our untreated wounds because we refuse (are terrified) to expose these painful stories to those around us, even though doing so can begin the healing process. As a result, our wounds either fester and grow bigger or heal poorly, leaving the emotional equivalent of ugly, permanent scars and chronic pain. In either case, the wound continues to adversely impact us and our relationships. We choose the familiar pain of chronic wound over the risk of the temporary pain associated with healing. That is, we choose to leave the Teenage Mutant Ninja Turtles towel in place and the wound goes untreated.

In our well-meaning efforts to guard our hearts from the terror of exposure and the threat of worsening pain, we also guard against doing the rest of our lives better. A quote attributed to psychotherapist Virginia Satir captured this tension well: "Most people prefer the certainty of misery over the misery of uncertainty."

As you contemplate telling your story at a deeper level, ask yourself, Am I ready to let go of the certainty of misery and move toward the hope of healing that comes from the uncertain, unguarded, towel-less world? It's my hope that you will take the risk, face the exposure, and initiate the healing of those wounded parts of your story (large and small). I hope you'll choose to pull back your towel and let the light of truth shine on your wounds. I hope you'll take the risk of sharing those tender stories with others who can help initiate the healing that only exposure can bring.

If you answer yes, you might be struggling with the next question: How much of my story do I tell? Allow me to respond by switching from a medical analogy to a financial one. Think of your story as a precious, valuable resource that you want to manage and steward responsibly and well, just as you'd want to manage your money responsibly and well. Those who are too free with their money soon find themselves with insufficient funds when they need them most. Those who are too stingy ensure neither they nor those around them experience the benefit of their resources.

You are the world's expert on your story, and you have total control of how much or how little you share. My invitation to you as you engage others in the sharing of your story is to take small risks and share up to where you feel comfortable. Don't let yourself feel pressured to share, and don't overshare with people who aren't safe. That's neither wise nor kind.

Your story is your legacy. All the good and bad things you've been through, all you've experienced and accomplished, are worth sharing. They can help and encourage others. And sharing them is helpful to you. Psychologist Daniel Taylor observed: "If you want to share your legacy—and you should want to—you must tell us your stories, because your legacy is embedded in them. Tell the stories of failure and pain as well as those of success and gladness."[1]

## POSITIVE AND NEGATIVE

Some of us like to emphasize the positive. These people see the glass as half full and tend to have an optimistic outlook on life. They remember primarily the good times and focus on the stuff that went well. There are many upsides to this temperament. These optimists (my wife included) are generally happy people and others like to be around them.

Others of us (myself included) prefer to focus on the negative. We see the glass as half empty and tend to have a more pessimistic outlook on life. We remember primarily the things that have gone wrong in the past and are determined to prevent them from happening again. We are often better scenario planners and problem solvers than our more optimistic brothers and sisters, whom we probably view as naive. Pessimists (or *realists*, as I like to think of us) may not be as cheery as our optimistic counterparts, but we are reliable and ready for whatever life brings.

When it comes to telling the whole of our stories, it makes sense that many *optimists* struggle to talk about the hard parts. Conversely, many *realists* tend to overlook the beautiful parts. It's important to know which type of person you are so you can be sure to get whatever help you might need to tell the other half of your story, the part that does not come naturally. You must tell a balanced account of your story or else you inadvertently lead others—and yourself—astray.

For example, if the only moments from my childhood I ever shared with you were the happy and productive ones (and there were many), you would likely characterize my childhood as positive and fortunate. You would assume I must have substantial positive consequences from my childhood and be grateful for my upbringing. And you would be correct. They would all be true. This version of my story is accurate—but it is not complete.

If this is the only version of my story I tell, you would miss out on hearing about the harder parts, the negative inputs that contributed to my messages of the wound. And I would miss out on the benefit of processing those negative parts of my story with you. As a result, I would be stuck with either denying the negative consequences in my life or being bewildered and imprisoned by them.

Typically, when we tell only the positive parts of our story, our motivations are good. We want to protect our family or others who wounded us, and we don't want to blame or be whiners. Both of these goals are noble. But it's important that we tell the hard parts along with the good *and* that we not blame or whine in the process.

Now imagine that the only experiences I shared with you were the painful or negative ones. If you heard nothing but the times when I was hurt or belittled by my father, neighbor, coach, and so on, you'd likely characterize my childhood as negative and painful. Certainly, if I told you select stories from my childhood, you would likely feel some sadness for me (as my mentor did). But just as the solely positive version of my story is accurate but incomplete, so is the solely negative version. If I told only the harder parts of my story, I'd be guilty of telling an imbalanced version, and I'd be disloyal to reality and to those who have wounded me along the way.

When we tell only the painful parts of our stories, we run the risk of trying to blame our family or other people for our problems. We risk portraying ourselves solely as victims and fail to take responsibility for our contributions and consequences. When we blame or shift the focus from ourselves to others, we miss out on the redemption that comes from stewarding our stories well by telling both the good and the bad. This is why having a balanced view of our stories is so important. Don't overlook the lovely parts and don't minimize the hard parts.

Your story is your prized possession. When you share your journey with others, it is a treasured gift to both you and your hearer. Please share your story wisely and be a mindful and careful listener in return to the stories of others. This give-and-take of such precious cargo will be healing for all who participate.

# For Reflection

Spend some time reflecting on the questions below by journaling your responses. Then, if you are comfortable, share your observations with someone who is safe and trustworthy (a close friend, a therapist, or a significant other).

- As you look over the table you filled out on page 175, what areas surprised you? Why?
- Describe how an event in one quadrant or dimension of your life substantially impacted you in one or more of the other quadrants.
- When you find yourself nervous about sharing parts of your story with a safe person, why do you think that is the case? What are the thoughts or concerns that go through your mind?

# NINE

# Expressive Writing

Having a traumatic experience was certainly bad for people in many ways, but people who had a trauma and kept that traumatic experience secret were much worse off.

—James Pennebaker, *Expressive Writing*

Marie was stuck. Everyone knew it. Her partner. Her friends. Her therapists. Marie truly did have a terrible childhood. After her father was laid off and unable to find work, the family lost their home, and Marie, her two younger sisters, and her parents went to live with her maternal grandparents.

Marie's mother and father both found low-paying jobs and left the girls with their grandparents. Grandma was critical, demanding, and verbally abusive to the girls, and she was especially hard on Marie. As a result, Marie, now a thirty-three-year-old mother and accountant, still has nightmares from those days at Grandma's house. She struggles with food issues and alcohol abuse. She's been in many support groups over the years and has told her story to multiple therapists, but she only seems to be getting worse.

The extra glasses of wine Marie drinks after dinner and the increasing insomnia have both taken their toll. Oversleeping, arriving late for work, and overdrinking at a restaurant meeting with clients just cost her yet another job.

Marie has told stories about her childhood to many people over the years. In terms of her willingness to process her past, it appeared she was taking good steps. And yet she remains stuck. What's going wrong?

Before you dive headfirst into joining a story group or spending long evenings sharing your story with others, here are a few words of caution: not all sharing is therapeutic. Psychologists and social scientists have recognized that not all expressions of processing our past are productive and bring healing. Research reveals that some methods of sharing or reliving your story can actually set back your progress.

Let's start by exploring a common unhelpful type of processing.

## RUMINATION: UNHELPFUL STORYTELLING

When our storytelling keeps us preoccupied with and perpetually reliving the same hurtful issue, we have left the realm of helpful storytelling. In fact, not only is such preoccupation not helpful, it actually makes matters worse. Researchers call this destructive type of story processing *rumination*, and they have discovered it can contribute to a variety of physical, emotional, and relational harms. Ruminating is when we repeatedly stew or linger on the hurtful thing that took place and how bad we feel about it. The memory of that incident gets stuck in our minds and repeats like a broken record.

Theologian Jerry Sittser commented on this phenomenon in the book *A Grace Disguised*, which chronicles the tragic story of losing his mother, wife, and child in a drunk-driving accident. In this important book, Sittser noted that ruminating on the memory of a traumatic incident "makes a person sick by projecting the same scene of pain into the soul day after day, as if it were a videotape that never stops. . . . That repetition pollutes the soul."[1]

In 2008, Yale professor Susan Nolen-Hoeksema and her colleagues published "Rethinking Rumination," a fascinating review article that explores the adverse impact of rumination.[2] Drawing from the findings of more than two hundred academic research papers, these experts reported that resentment and rumination can cause considerable harm. The authors named the following clinically verified, potentially negative consequences of rumination:

- Depression
- Anxiety
- Binge eating/drinking
- Poor problem-solving
- Self-harm
- Hopelessness
- Pessimism
- Self-criticism
- Dependency
- Neediness
- Prolonged distress
- Clingy interpersonal style
- Aggressive tendencies

Clearly, we want to avoid rumination. So how can we process and tell our stories without getting stuck in rumination?

Fortunately, research supports a helpful strategy called *expressive writing*. It's a tool I have benefited from and highly recommend.

## EXPRESSIVE WRITING

Expressive writing is a simple but scientifically validated means of recounting some of the scenes from your past in a way that leads to physical, emotional, and behavioral healing. Individuals who have used this practice report improvements in their objective understanding of the story elements they process, as well as their ability to recalibrate and reinterpret these events.

This important therapeutic technique was developed several decades ago by James W. Pennebaker, a professor and social psychologist at the University of Texas at Austin. He recognized an emotional benefit that comes from writing about a painful story in a prescribed fashion.[3] Pennebaker's early research validated what many already knew to be true; namely, we tend to get better when we write and talk about our painful experiences. The clinically demonstrated benefits of expressive writing include:

- *Improved physical health:* improvements in blood pressure, arthritis, irritable bowel, asthma, liver disease, and immune function
- *Improved emotional health:* decreased symptoms of PTSD, depression, anxiety, and an improved sense of well-being
- *Improved personal behaviors:* better sleep, work attendance, athletic performance, memory, reemployment after job loss, and student grade point averages

Pennebaker's early recipe for expressive writing asked participants to write uninterrupted, twenty minutes a day for four consecutive days. Recent research has studied some variations and additions to this original formula. Some found benefits in writing once a week for at least four weeks as opposed to writing daily for at least four days. Others found similar benefits in dictating one's story into a voice recorder rather than writing it out. Whether written or spoken, what worked in all cases was putting words to one's experience consistently and uninterrupted.

I'm going to walk you through the steps of Pennebaker's method, but first I want to address two questions that often arise when I present expressive writing in workshops and use it with my coaching clients: How does expressive writing avoid rumination and how does it help?

## How Does Expressive Writing Avoid Rumination?

This is an important question, and the good news is that scientific research on Pennebaker's method provides a compelling answer.

Scholars discovered that when writers simply narrate *what* happened to them, expressive writing is less useful and can lead to rumination. But when writers explore *why* the events happened, their expressive writing demonstrates significant therapeutic benefit.[4] According to Pennebaker and others, one way to accomplish this is to write what happened from the perspective of others in the story or from a bird's-eye view as an objective narrator. For example, you might write in the third person, as if you were an uninvolved news reporter simply capturing the events. Taking a more distant perspective allows you to be inquisitive about the scene, and you'll likely see things you hadn't noticed before.

I often encourage people to start their first day of writing from whatever perspective they feel like, which is often first person. This means using "I" and writing about the event as you experienced it, including any strong emotions. For example, on day one you might write, "I can't believe Terry betrayed me like this. I'm so mad!" Then, on subsequent days, you could shift the perspective from *what* happened to *why* it happened, that is, be curious about what may have been going on behind the scenes. For example, "I wonder why Terry did this. Why did he betray me? Could it be that . . ."

Writing about why something happened requires curiosity and a shifting of perspective. And the research is clear that the more we understand the why—the origins and meaning of painful or traumatic events—the more likely we are to experience healing. In his book *The End of Memory*, Miloslav Volf affirmed this dynamic: "Personal healing happens not so much by remembering traumatic events and their accompanying emotions as by *interpreting* memories and *inscribing* them into a larger pattern of meaning."[5]

I've found expressive writing to be extremely helpful in processing my own story. Like most people, I have a couple of scenes from my childhood that left their marks. If I were to write about one such story from an impartial news reporter's view, it might read like this:

> I see a little boy, maybe six or seven years old, in the barnyard of their farm. He's crying because he's being forced to do something he doesn't want to do. An angry man, his father, stands next to him. The father is laughing and mocking the son. His mother is also there. She looks conflicted, like she's not sure what to do.

After capturing the scene as a reporter, I would then move to curiosity and start writing my best answers to a whole bunch of why questions:

- Why is the father so angry?
- Why does the father want the boy to do this?
- What is going on inside the boy?
- Why is the father mocking and laughing at the boy?
- What is the mother feeling?
- Why isn't she helping the boy?
- What is she afraid of?

Writing from the perspective of an uninvolved observer rather than from the perspective of the scared boy gives me a new vantage point. It allows me to discover a deeper, more healing understanding of what happened that day.

Writing about why an event like this might have happened doesn't mean I will no longer feel sympathy for myself as the boy, nor does it legitimize my father's actions. The whole incident is still sad. But getting a deeper perspective through expressive writing helps me to understand my father, my mother, and myself better. It is a catalyst for me to heal and move on. Expressive writing significantly lessens the grip that hurtful stories like this one have on me—and their adverse effects in my life as an adult. I wish the same healing benefits for you.

Note the following important caveat: tools such as expressive writing are no substitute for the professional help required to deal with substantially traumatic stories. Those who have experienced such harm usually require the assistance of a professional therapist to achieve the breakthroughs and insights required for healing. If you have a history of trauma, expressive writing alone will not provide the intensive attention you need. Seeking out a certified therapist—particularly one credentialed in a mode of therapy called EMDR (eye movement desensitization and reprocessing)— remains an important resource in your healing journey.

## How Does Expressive Writing Help?

There are many theories about how expressive writing helps people heal from past harms. Here are the two hypotheses I find most compelling: exposure therapy and neural reorganizing.

**1. Exposure therapy:** Exposing someone to a troubling experience for the purpose of desensitizing them to it has long been used by social scientists to help their clients overcome disabling fears. Here's how it typically works.

Imagine I have a fear of snakes and I've turned to my therapist for help. She might first expose me to a photograph of a snake and ask me to hold the photo. Then she might take me into a room where a snake is contained in a secure glass cage. Next, I'm invited to approach and touch the glass. On a future visit, I may touch the snake in its tank. Eventually, I would actually hold the snake. Over time, my fear of snakes would have a less disabling power over me.

Exposure therapy has proven successful in helping people overcome all sorts of fears, process grief and loss, and—in the context of our stories—gain power over events or experiences that wounded them.

Our more painful experiences sometimes take on an identity of their own, deep in our psyches. Some experts believe that engaging the story in a controlled and paced reexposure—such as expressive writing for twenty minutes or retelling a story in a safe environment—can act as a form of exposure therapy, which reduces the destructive power it has over us. Over time, expressive writing allows us to have a more productive, healing relationship with the painful parts of our story.

**2. Neural reorganizing:** This theory is more complex and less well understood or defined by the therapeutic community. Some experts believe that some of our traumatic memories are inadequately processed and stored in our brains. Therefore, expressive writing aids in "memory system reconsolidation," a form of reorganizing memories.[6] This allows our brains to evaluate and store these memories in a more productive and manageable manner. As a result, we should experience fewer negative impacts, both consciously and subconsciously.

This is heady stuff. The best analogy I've come up with to describe this process is the relationship I have with the top drawer of my desk. (My apologies to neuroscientists and EMDR practitioners who may find this analogy a gross oversimplification.)

I have a habit of tossing the stuff in my pocket into the top drawer of my desk. All kinds of stuff. Even stuff that doesn't belong there. My top drawer is just the most convenient place to put stuff when I'm distracted or in a hurry. I repeatedly tell myself I will sort it out later, before it becomes a problem.

Eventually, however, it becomes a problem. My top drawer becomes a chaotic jumble of stuff, much of which I really don't need to keep and most of which belongs elsewhere—in another drawer or on a shelf or in a container with similar objects. Now, when I open the drawer, the stuff on top that doesn't belong there makes it difficult to find the stuff I need that does belong there. The longer my top drawer stays in this chaotic condition, the more stressed out I feel when I open it, which is many times a day.

I know if I don't do something about this drawer, it will become such a disorganized mess that I'll avoid it. In fact, I'll eventually start to dread opening it. Which means I miss out on the benefits of a well-stocked, organized top desk drawer.

To deal with this issue, I need to start the tedious process of pulling out each item in the drawer, inspecting it, and then doing one of three things with it:

1. Group it with similar items that may serve me in the future and put them all in another drawer of the desk.
2. Toss it.
3. Return it to my newly organized top drawer.

Once this process is completed, it's much less distressing to work at my desk and open my top drawer. The previously chaotically stored components may still trouble me, but because the elements in the drawer now have more order, they have less power over me. I now have easier access to all my stuff. In fact, opening the drawer after this reconsolidation is actually peaceful and pleasing.

A similar dynamic is at work when it comes to all the memories we've stuffed into our brains over the years, some of which are traumatic or painful. These painful memories need to be examined individually and then organized into their ideal space, that is, a place where we find greater insight about what happened to us.

Whether through exposure therapy (such as expressive writing) or through memory reorganizing or any other plausible explanations of why telling our story is beneficial, the unifying goal is to help us create order and meaning of those traumatizing stories. Finding meaning is central to healing our stories and writing a new plot. Academic and author Melissa Kelley captured this truth when she wrote: "Meaning, including theological meaning, helps to create order, sense, and purpose out of experiences and events that could otherwise seem random, nonsensical, disordered, or chaotic."[7]

This is not the same as trying to manufacture something good out of difficulty. And this is not about legitimizing another person's damaging behavior or minimizing the hurt they caused. Instead, it's about gaining the therapeutic benefits that come with the efforts to better understand the big picture.

Of course, we will never like the bad things that happened to us, but when we view them with greater insight and within a bigger picture of life, we will feel less helpless and imprisoned by them. Telling our stories, whether through sharing them with safe people or through writing about them, helps us rightsize our distorted beliefs about how we see ourselves, the world, and our place in it.

Now that we've explored what expressive writing is and addressed some common questions, I hope you're eager to give it a try. Get out a pen and journal or a laptop and prepare to write!

## FIVE STEPS FOR EXPRESSIVE WRITING

From my own experience and by observation, Pennebaker's original, clinically verified method of expressive writing seems to be the most efficient and effective strategy. It is certainly the most researched. I find his recommendation to write at least twenty minutes each day for no fewer than four days to be a strategy that is both maximally effective and minimally disruptive. What follows is my adaptation of Pennebaker's original method.

The process begins by identifying a hurt, a traumatic event, or an area of loss that is important to you, then writing about it. Below is how you should write:

1. *Write for four consecutive days:* You can write for as many consecutive days as you like, but be sure to write for *at least* four consecutive days to maximize the benefit. If you miss a day, no problem. Just start again and write for the next four consecutive days.

2. *Write continuously for at least twenty minutes each day:* Do this in a single sitting. Don't stop and take a break in the middle of your twenty minutes. Keep your pen or fingers moving. You can write for longer if you want but not shorter. If you go over twenty minutes one day, you still need to log your full twenty minutes the next day. The minutes don't carry over.

3. *Write only for yourself:* Don't plan on sharing what you write with others. No one but you needs to see what you write. Don't anticipate sending your writing to the person who hurt you. Don't worry about spelling. Don't worry about grammar. Don't worry about neatness. Don't worry about punctuation. Just capture your thoughts and feelings in one nonstop outpouring. When you're done, feel free to do what you would like with what you wrote. You can burn it, toss it, erase it, save it, and so on. The main value is in the process of expressing your thoughts into words.

4. *Be kind to yourself:* If you begin to feel worked up,

overwhelmed, or distressed, it's okay to stop. When you're ready, start again at day one.

5. *Don't be surprised if, at first, you feel worse afterward:* Many social scientists with experience in expressive writing report that people often feel sad or melancholy immediately after a session of writing. That's the bad news. The good news is that this phenomenon is short-lived, often resolving in thirty minutes or less. And those low feelings are typically followed by a substantial and prevailing sense of well-being or improvement. Then, over the ensuing weeks, writers feel much better, even if they wrote for only four days. Healing has begun.

When I first tried expressive writing some years ago, the first two days were a bit distressing. At the end of my first session, I wrote, "Great. Now I feel worse. This clearly isn't working." And yet, after the fourth day of writing, I began to notice a shift, a slow progress toward improvement.

If you want to give expressive writing a go but aren't sure where to start, here are some prompts to jump-start your thinking:

- Where did the event(s) take place? (Describe the setting.)
- When did the event(s) take place?
- Who were the people involved?
- Why were they involved?
- What triggered the episode?
- What happened?
- How did you feel then?
- What have been the ripple effects of that event for you? For others?

- Why is this event important for you to understand and tell?
- How are you different today because of this event?
- What have you learned from this event?

Remember that one of the main objectives of expressive writing is to help you make sense of a troubling experience or event. With increased understanding and insight, you can incorporate that experience into the bigger and more coherent story of your life.

The journey of understanding your story and mining insights from it help you identify your distorted beliefs without leaving you stuck in a painful cycle of rumination. Once this essential task is underway, you have the freedom you need to move forward so you can do the rest of your life better.

## For Reflection

Practice expressive writing by identifying a troubling or painful part of your story and writing about it using the five steps presented in this chapter (pages 197–199). Then use the questions on the next page to process your experience with a trusted person, a friend, or a therapist. As you practice expressive writing, remember that you're not going to share what you wrote with others. Feel free, however, to share any observations, insights, or impacts of your writing.

- What is the difference between rumination and productive sharing?
- What sort of gentle redirection language do you suggest you and your trusted person use when the other is slipping into rumination?
- After completing a session of expressive writing, what new insights have you gained related to the episodes you wrote about?

# TEN

# Further Steps on the Journey

Our story will gain momentum and depth only to the
degree that we honestly embrace both loss and fear.

—Dan Allender, *To Be Told*

This would be a great job if it weren't for the people!

—Just about everyone

Early on in my journey of story work, I was encouraged by how
rapidly I was able to make some significant progress in untan-
gling my story and finding healing from past hurts. But then my
growth seemed to hit a plateau. *Is this it?* I wondered. *Is this as
much healing as I can do? How would I move beyond this plateau?*

It takes intentionality and time to heal past hurts and make
lasting changes in how we relate to others. Plateaus are normal. In
fact, having now walked alongside hundreds of individuals doing
this type of story work, I now realize that my experience—early

progress followed by a plateau—is a nearly universal experience. Expect and welcome the plateaus. It means you're doing great work and you're right on track.

Have you hit a plateau yet? If not, don't be surprised if you join me there, along with countless others. And when you do, there's good news! It's time to augment the journey by employing new behavioral patterns that invigorate you and perpetuate your success in writing a new plot. These practices will help you rise beyond the plateau and find true healing.

Social scientists have identified three practices proven to facilitate tremendous healing and relational well-being among those who practice them. These practices—each of them rather intuitive—create the most powerful healing sequence I know of when practiced together. Let's take a brief look at each in this last chapter together:

1. Grieve the losses.
2. Forgive the wrongs.
3. Express gratitude for the rest.

I could write enough to fill another book about each task. In fact, there are already a number of great books on these topics that are worth reading.[1] For now, I'll cover the *what* and the *why* of each practice and how these practices together can make a huge difference in healing our stories.

Before we dive in, allow me to respond to a question that often arises at this point: If these three practices (grief, forgiveness, and gratitude) are such amazing pathways to healing, why can't I just skip all that family-of-origin work and go straight into working on them? In other words, why bother doing the work of processing the messages of the wound, negative consequences, and all the rest? Fair question.

My response is, recall all the hard work required to

- gain clarity on the positive and negative inputs from your story;
- understand how your negative inputs leave you at risk for negative consequences and automatic responses in your relationships;
- connect your distorted messages to their corresponding consequences; and
- rewrite the distorted ways you see yourself, the world, and your place in it.

If you don't do the hard work first, you'll engage the topics of grief, forgiveness, and gratitude without proper context. You'll still be operating out of your old, distorted views of yourself and others. And without the insights you've gained by doing the work, you won't be able to make the practices maximally effective and healing. Instead, you'll apply the wrong treatment to your aches and pursue solutions to the wrong dilemmas.

However, when you do the work and develop new insights into your past, you'll experience what I call the *virtuous loop effect*. It works something like this:

There is a synergistic relationship between understanding your story and engaging in grief, forgiveness, and gratitude. Once you begin grieving the wounds of your past, you'll be more able to forgive those who've harmed you and be grateful for the beautiful parts of your story, which in turn fuels new insights into your story. Greater insights into your story means you'll gain *even more* benefit from grief, forgiveness, and gratitude. And so the loop continues.

It is only in the relational work associated with the three practices that we find ultimate healing from the wounds of our past. Psychologist Henry Cloud captured this reality when he wrote: "Distorted thinking was learned in the context of relationship, and that is the only place where it can be unlearned."[2]

## GRIEVE THE LOSSES

Grief is a natural, necessary response to loss. It ushers in myriad emotions, such as depression, sadness, hopelessness, and anger. Author C. S. Lewis expressed my own experience with grief when he wrote: "No one ever told me that grief felt so like fear."[3] It can be a real sucker punch. It takes your breath away and refuses to be ignored. "Grieve," said poet Nayyireh Waheed, "so that you can be free to feel something else."[4]

The shortest (and only) way out of the discomfort of grief is to work your way through it. Grief is one of the most difficult feelings to experience and express, which is why many of us tend to avoid it. But if we shortcut grief, we won't be able to move on to forgiveness and gratitude. Grief comes first.

Grief is multifaceted and unique to you: the type of loss you experienced and the season of life you're in. There is no single correct way to grieve—no perfect stages, no correct path, no playbook—that works for everyone. It's often two steps forward, one step back. Because grief is so uncomfortable, many people work hard to avoid the experience through denial, anesthesia, or distraction. But those strategies only prolong their suppressed grief. For healing to begin, we must face the discomfort and grieve. The only way out is through it.

Begin by naming the loss. Until we get clear on the nature and depth of what we've lost, we cannot really begin to grieve. Many resist naming the loss because it makes the loss feel final or real. It's hard to face our new normal, so we avoid grief in the vain hope that we can somehow redo yesterday differently or better. But until we name our loss, we have no hope of freeing ourselves from its pain. True healing begins with grief over a specific loss, not through generalized sadness over a nebulous loss we refuse to name. As author Melissa Kelley stated, "Hope begins with reality."[5]

The expressive writing tool we engaged in the previous chapter is particularly helpful when it comes to naming the reality and depth of loss, especially when we're grieving the losses from our negative inputs, beliefs, and consequences. Keep in mind that individuals with similar negative inputs will not necessarily experience the same type of loss. We each experience loss uniquely, and there are as many reactions to a loss as there are individuals in this world.

What's your unique experience with loss? It will be worth your while to wrestle with any specific loss that is hard for you to process or move past.

Here are a few examples of loss experienced by my friends and coaching clients:

- Randy was a rather shy, awkward child. As a result, he was teased and bullied at school. Now he is learning to grieve the fact that he is not comfortable in crowds and has never had many deep friendships.
- Sara grew up with parents who expected her to be the best at everything: grades, sports, competitions, popularity, and more. Because of her perfectionism and workaholism as an adult, she's never satisfied. She's lonely and sad that she has never made room for a stable romantic partner. Now she is learning to grieve her inability to feel the peace and accomplishment that comes from a job well done.
- Alec had several abusive men in his family. He grew up with an intense distrust of others (particularly men) and has issues with anger that hurt his relationships at home and work. Now he is learning to grieve the loss that comes with not having any benevolent male role models or friends throughout his adult life. He is also grieving the financial strain and loss of reputation that come with repeatedly losing jobs because of his anger.
- Jules grew up in a home with significant substance abuse and instability. Now she is learning to grieve her inability to feel safe and function well in a family. She is also grieving the losses associated with her own subsequent substance abuse: relationships, money, vocational progress, and health.

Don't fast-forward past grief. Be patient with yourself. Grief is a slow, irregular process. It doesn't happen overnight. We don't get *over* our loss; we get *on* with it.

Grief is one of the most important and least practiced

disciplines when it comes to our emotional health. As Karen Maroda observed, "The patients who seem to change the most are those who are capable of deep grieving."[6] Be among those who change the most.

## FORGIVE THE WRONGS

Over the last two decades there has been a great deal of research on the topic of forgiveness. The vast majority of these studies support the statistically significant emotional and physical benefits associated with being more forgiving. Forgiveness "is the only means to overcome hate and condemnation and proceed with the business of growing and loving," noted Paul W. Coleman.[7]

Check out some of the empirically validated benefits of forgiveness:

**Emotional improvements**
- Emotional stability
- Sense of purpose/meaning
- Improved mood, fewer episodes of depression
- Greater self-acceptance
- Less anxiety, stress, and hostility
- Better anger management

**Physical improvements**
- Fewer sick days
- Better immune function, less illness
- Decreased alcohol and drug abuse
- Improved blood pressure

- Less coronary heart disease
- Greater life expectancy

The benefits of a forgiving heart are not limited to the individual who forgives. Forgiveness also leads to profound relational, social, and cultural benefits. In international hotbeds of hurt and anger, such as apartheid South Africa and Israel–Palestine, forgiveness movements have led to dramatic improvements in relationships among participants.[8]

Research is clear on the myriad benefits of forgiveness, both individually and as a society. Sadly, the converse is also true. Boundless volumes of empirical data demonstrate that unforgiveness has profoundly destructive implications socially, emotionally, spiritually, and relationally. In chapter 9, we discussed the adverse impact of rumination. The problem of rumination is directly associated with the condition of unforgiveness. When we dwell on hurts and wounds from the past without inviting forgiveness, we remain stuck in the pain of those hurts. When we choose not to forgive, we not only miss out on the massive benefits of forgiveness, but we also submit ourselves to ongoing emotional pain, which sabotages the process of healing the broken parts of our story.

When we forgive, we are declaring that the infractions of the other person are no longer kept in our ledger of wrongs. We no longer expect any compensation, ownership, or repentance from the other person.[9] Specifically, we release the hurt and let go of any expectations we've held on to that keep us bound to the person who harmed us. Henry Cloud drove that point home in *Changes That Heal*: "Bitterness and holding a grudge will forever connect you to your abuser."[10]

I don't want to minimize the discomfort that comes when

confronted with the prospect of forgiving someone who has caused significant harm. Forgiveness is difficult for a number of reasons. However, oftentimes we resist forgiveness because we don't really understand what it is. In fact, many people overcome the barriers they face when struggling to forgive once they get clear on what forgiveness is *not*.

Following are five things forgiveness is *not*:

1. *Forgiveness is not forgetting:* We can forgive someone's actions and still remember the painful infraction. We can stop expecting anything from the other person and keep reasonable safeguards in place as trust is rebuilt. "The stupid neither forgive nor forget; the naive forgive and forget; the wise forgive but do not forget," observed Thomas Szasz.[11] I couldn't agree more.

2. *Forgiveness is not for the weak:* There have been times when I knew the most productive step in a relationship would be to forgive the other person—and yet I didn't. This was not because I was strong; it was because I lacked the humility and courage that forgiveness requires. I love this quote by Mahatma Gandhi: "The weak can never forgive. Forgiveness is the attribute of the strong."[12]

3. *Forgiveness is not reconciliation:* The process of forgiveness doesn't necessarily mean the relationship will be reconciled. Reconciliation, or the resumption of compatibility and relationship, requires forgiveness *plus* the presence of trust-building safeguards. You can't have reconciliation without forgiveness, but you can forgive someone without reconciling with them. (With unrepentant, unsafe people, this is often the wisest choice.)

4. *Forgiveness is not restoration:* We mistakenly believe that to forgive someone essentially means to let them get away with it. Nope. While restoration of what was lost or resuming past relationship may be ideal outcomes, they aren't necessary for forgiveness. You can choose to forgive someone without restoration, but you can't have restoration without forgiveness.

5. *Forgiveness is not dependent on the other person being sorry:* We may never hear the words "I'm sorry" from someone who harmed us. Perhaps they have passed away, are unrepentant, or are simply unaware of how they hurt us. Never hearing the satisfying words "I'm sorry" may add to our hurt, but it doesn't keep us from extending forgiveness. Forgiveness is a solo sport. It's something we do for ourselves to break free from the hold the other person's actions have on us. It allows us to no longer be bound to the perpetrator or the consequences of their actions. When we forgive, we release the other person so we can be free.

Once again, the tool that I and many others I've coached have found useful in the task of forgiveness is the practice of expressive writing covered in chapter 9.

## EXPRESS GRATITUDE FOR THE REST

There are enormous emotional, physical, spiritual, and relational benefits to embracing a habit of gratitude, even short-term gratitude for small blessings in life.

Taking note of the things in our lives for which we can be grateful especially helps us become more consistently cognizant of two important realities:

- Even when life is difficult, we typically have much good to celebrate in our lives.
- Most of that good comes from beyond ourselves—from people, experiences, and opportunities. This realization helps us celebrate things such as nature, weather, art, and music.

Researcher Robert Emmons is probably the most recognized expert on the topic of gratitude with multiple published studies and at least five books highlighting the results of his decades of research. In one of his studies, Emmons teamed up with Michael McCullough, one of the foremost experts on forgiveness, to publish a study demonstrating the positive impact of gratitude on numerous factors, including physical well-being, sleep, mood, and anxiety.[13]

Additional studies have demonstrated that even the periodic practice of gratitude can lead to growth and improvements in the following:

- Empathy
- Alertness
- Energy
- Joy
- Helpfulness toward others
- Physical health
- Exercise
- Sleep
- Optimism
- Happiness
- Social skills
- Eliminating loneliness
- Lessening depression

Any of these proven benefits of gratitude certainly should inspire us to implement gratitude-building practices into our lives. But most relevant to our discussion here is the finding that gratitude is beneficial as we heal from past hurts. In the book *Gratitude Works!* Emmons highlights studies that demonstrate that the practice of gratitude facilitates

- an improved ability to cope with stress;
- a sense of closure in traumatic memories; and
- bolstered feelings of self-worth and self-confidence.[14]

Even when we know all the benefits of gratitude, it doesn't come naturally for many of us—myself included. In order to experience gratitude consistently, I need daily prompts to help me make gratitude a practice rather than a fluke. When I first began pursuing more gratitude in my life, I added reminders to my Google calendar to send me prompts throughout the day to identify something for which I was grateful. Adding each prompt only took a few seconds, but the regularity of those prompts has definitely increased my gratitude levels and improved my outlook on life.

Maximize the powerful benefits of gratitude by using whatever prompts, habits, or systems you need to practice gratitude throughout your day. Something as simple as a sticky note in your car or at your workplace can be a meaningful reminder that you have many things in your life for which to be grateful.

Here are some additional practices that have been empirically validated as effective in helping people become more grateful:

- Write a thank-you note.
- Keep a gratitude journal.

- Count your blessings regularly.
- Carry a remember stone.

Allow me to expound on two of these practices that have been most helpful to me and the people I've coached.

### Keep a Gratitude Journal

Gratitude journaling is simply writing out specific things for which you are grateful. If you develop a regular habit of journaling, you'll soon notice many of the proven benefits, as well as an increased sense of feeling more grateful overall. Most researchers who've explored gratitude journaling suggest developing the habit of writing every day.

One nuance I've found relates to how much to write about each thing I'm grateful for. When I first tried keeping a gratitude journal, each entry was simply a gratitude list:

1. My wife
2. My job
3. My friend Andy

Better than nothing perhaps, but much less effective than journaling more specifically. So I started writing more. Instead of stopping at "my wife," I wrote, "I'm grateful that my wife preps the coffee maker each night so that the coffee is ready in the morning when I get up." Instead of "my friend Andy," I wrote, "I'm grateful that Andy is so encouraging to me. I am grateful for the kind email he sent yesterday."

Being specific increases my gratitude when I encounter those specific things or people I've written about. It also reminds me of so many other things I'm grateful for throughout the day. If you start a gratitude journal and initially feel like you don't have much to say, get specific. You'll be surprised how much more effective your journaling becomes when you name the details of your gratitude.

### Carry a Remember Stone

When I feel my gratitude levels slipping (which, sadly, is often), I carry one of my remember stones.[15] I keep it in the front pocket of my pants and find myself holding it often throughout the day. Each time I touch this stone, I am reminded to stop and be grateful for something or someone. Typically, at that moment, I think of no fewer than three things for which I am grateful. Most times I include my wife, kids, and grandkids. Other times I express gratitude for my job, my friends, or the abundance my family and I possess (specifically that we live in a house with air conditioning, ample food, and clean water). The remember stone actually works!

## LIGHTENING YOUR STEPS

Here is the paradox of the three disciplines of grieving, forgiving, and practicing gratitude: all three can be difficult to practice on their own, but practicing them together can make our lives easier—and much better.

I'm consistently encouraged by the reports I get from people who, after reluctantly committing to making regular efforts to practice the three disciplines, feel as if a giant burden has been lifted from their shoulders. They feel liberated. This has been my experience as well. Try it. I believe you'll find your steps getting lighter on this journey toward healing and the relationships you want.

## For Reflection

Process where you are with grief, forgiveness, and gratitude by journaling your responses to the questions below, and then share your observations with a trusted person.

- Which one of the three practices comes easiest for you? Which is hardest? Why do you think this is so?
- *Grieve the losses:* You cannot redo yesterday and, sadly, you cannot undo the harmful experiences that pepper your early years. But you can name them and allow yourself to grieve them. Which negative inputs or beliefs (identified in chapter 5) most need to be grieved? What specifically have you lost as a result of those experiences?
- *Forgive the wrongs:* How would you describe your experiences with forgiveness overall? Is there someone you feel you need to forgive in connection with the negative inputs or beliefs you identified? What specifically do you need to forgive? (You may benefit from processing this

with a therapist and/or a trusted friend and by using expressive writing.)

- *Express gratitude for the rest:* Briefly review the positive inputs, beliefs, and consequences you identified in chapter 4. For what and for whom are you especially grateful? Be specific. Identify concrete ways you can express gratitude for the positive parts of your story, which have formed and nurtured some of the most beautiful parts of who you are.

# Do the Rest of Your Life Better

At this writing, September and I have been married thirty-five years, and I am sure she would agree when I tell you those thirty-five have encompassed the happiest *twenty-seven* years of our lives. We both regret the destructive patterns of relating we brought to our marriage and parenting, way back in 1984. But we didn't know what we didn't know. I was unaware of the subconscious, distorted messages that hindered so many of my relationships. I wish I knew then what you and I know now. It is possible to change those unproductive patterns. We really can do the rest of our lives better!

Today, September and I enjoy the sweetest marriage of anyone we know. And this change came about when I learned the principles shared in this book.

I started with some uncomfortable soul-searching and asking others in my life (friends, family, therapists, mentors) to mirror back to me what they saw. How did I hinder our relationship? Had I harmed them in some way? Their responses and my own reflection revealed some common themes, and I quickly identified a list of behaviors that needed to change. But I knew I needed more than behavior modification. It would take more than sheer willpower to conquer these long-ingrained patterns.

So next I compiled an honest, thorough understanding of

the negative inputs from my earlier years (key words: *honest* and *thorough*). I wrote everything down, even if I didn't understand whether it was connected to my current negative consequences. Thoroughness and honesty are required if we are going to succeed in the next—and most critical—step in the process: understanding my specific messages of the wound.

The process of gaining clarity on my unique messages of the wound took more time, patience, and trial and error than I would have guessed. The message "People will betray and discard you" was a surprise to me. I'd never stated this message out loud, and I really hadn't even consciously played it in my mind. But there it was, hovering as the backdrop of my psyche. I quickly realized it was the driver behind my pattern of withdrawing when at risk of being hurt or scared.

This recurring defensive pattern caused hurt and confusion to September and anyone else who wanted a closer relationship with me. When I understood the various distorted ways I (mis)interpreted everything around me, I was ready to heal.

Once I clearly understood my messages of the wound, it was much easier to catch myself when I was behaving as if those distorted, false messages were true. This awareness escalated my progress toward emotional and relational health.

Letting others in on my journey helped immensely as well. I asked trusted friends and loved ones to tell me whenever my behavior seemed tied to my old messages, so I could instead choose new, truthful messages. Over time those new ways of relating have become habits. While I still slip up and revert to old messages at times, for the most part my relationships today are characterized by positive consequences driven by positive beliefs about myself, the world, and my place in it.

If this journey sounds daunting to you, I invite you to take a deep breath and pace yourself. Be patient and kind to yourself as you take one step at a time. This isn't a race, and you won't walk through it perfectly. But you will make real and lasting progress. If you're like me, you'll fumble and get sidetracked here and there. Not only is that okay, it's perfectly normal. Don't get discouraged. Just refocus on why you're taking this journey: to do the rest of your life better.

With the concepts and tools you have learned in this book, the behavioral changes you want to make are within your grasp. You can change those patterns that adversely impact your relational, vocational, and romantic connections. You really can grow and heal from the past. And you can leave a legacy of healthy relationships for the generations that follow you.

It's my hope and prayer that you continue to make small progress every day on your journey toward understanding your story. May you recognize, refute, and replace every distorted message that comes your way. Go slow. Give yourself grace. Do the work.

You really can change yourself, the world, and your place in it. It's never too late to do life better by building better relationships.

# Acknowledgments

Nearly everything I know about relationships I learned from working alongside thousands of courageous individuals who have come to my business, church, or office for emotional and relational guidance. I learned from each and every one of them. I am forever grateful for their willingness to share their lives with me.

A number of people read early drafts of this manuscript and offered important suggestions that made the book stronger. Thank you to Sue Hood, Andy Hartman, Scott Browning, Scott Gibson, Janice Troeger, and Heather Larson.

A special thanks to this book's editor, Christine Anderson. Many of the structural decisions and choice phrases in this book were her ideas. Thanks to my team at HarperCollins/Thomas Nelson—Jessica Wong, Sujin Hong, and Ed Curtis—for their phenomenal support, skill, and encouragement. And a special thanks to my agent, Chris Ferebee, who has been a wise guiding force in bringing this book to publication.

# Notes

### Chapter 1: Story: Why Bother?
1. The National Board Exam's cyanide question is almost always related to the telltale sign of acute cyanide toxicity, which is described as a "bitter almond odor" to the patient's breath. As part of my initial exam, I had removed the patient's oxygen bag and sniffed his endotracheal-tube emissions. Nada. No almond smell. I had others in the room sniff as well. Nothing. It turns out only a minority of people are genetically endowed with the ability to recognize that specific smell. And none of us in the ER that day was so endowed.
2. William Faulkner, *Requiem for a Nun* (New York: Random House, 1950), 73.

### Chapter 2: What Is Story?
1. Daniel Taylor's book *Tell Me a Story: The Life-Shaping Power of Our Stories* (St. Paul, MN: Bog Walk Press, 2005) and Dan Allender's book *To Be Told: God Invites You to Coauthor Your Future* (Colorado Springs: WaterBrook, 2005) are "must reads" for anyone wanting to learn more about the topic of story.
2. Louis Cozolino, *Why Therapy Works: Using Our Minds to Change Our Brains*, Norton Series on Interpersonal Neurobiology (New York: Norton, 2015), 25.
3. Taylor, *Tell Me a Story*, 13.

### Chapter 3: Characters: Understanding the Who of Your Story

1. Monica McGoldrick and Randy Gerson, *Genograms in Family Assessment* (New York: Norton, 1986).
2. If you search "genogram" online, you'll discover there are a number of acceptable ways to draw one. You'll also discover how detailed and potentially complicated you can make the process, if you are so inclined. For our purposes, we will take a fairly uncomplicated route.
3. The Centers for Disease Control (www.cdc.gov) reports that nearly 25 percent of American women will experience some form of intimate partner violence, rape, and/or stalking in their lifetime. This translates to nearly five million American women experiencing domestic violence every year. Similarly, the CDC reports that nearly 25 percent of Americans binge and/or excessively drink alcohol each month.

### Chapter 4: Positive Plot Points: Maximizing the Best Parts of Your Story

1. Louis Cozolino, *Why Therapy Works: Using Our Minds to Change Our Brains*, Norton Series on Interpersonal Neurobiology (New York: Norton, 2015), 249.
2. Daniel Taylor, *Tell Me a Story: The Life-Shaping Power of Our Stories* (St. Paul, MN: Bog Walk Press, 2005), 1.

### Chapter 5: Negative Plot Points: Healing the Hard Parts of Your Story

1. Arthur W. Frank, *Letting Stories Breathe: A Socio-Narratology* (Chicago: University of Chicago Press, 2010), 8.
2. Timothy D. Wilson, *Redirect: Changing the Stories We Live By* (New York: Little, Brown Spark, 2011), 9.

### Chapter 6: Automatic Responses: Taming the Reactions from Your Past

1. I apologize to any neuroscientists reading this book. My anatomy description is dramatically oversimplified for the purposes

of distinguishing the *protective* neuromechanisms from the *prosocial* neuromechanisms. If I were to provide a more robust description here, I would highlight other limbic structures, such as the right insula. A fantastic resource for a more empirically detailed treatment is David Schnarch, *Brain Talk: How Mind Mapping Brain Science Can Change Your Life and Everyone in It* (Scotts Valley, CA: CreateSpace, 2018).

2. Mark Goulston, *Just Listen: Discover the Secret to Getting Through to Absolutely Anyone* (New York: American Management Association, 2010), 15.

3. Joseph LeDoux, quoted in Brent Atkinson, *Emotional Intelligence in Couples Therapy: Advances from Neurobiology and the Science of Intimate Relationships* (New York: Norton, 2005), 25.

4. Atkinson, *Emotional Intelligence in Couples Therapy*, 25–26.

5. Louis Cozolino, *Why Therapy Works: Using Our Minds to Change Our Brains*, Norton Series on Interpersonal Neurobiology (New York: Norton, 2015), 61.

6. Andrew Newberg and Mark Robert Waldman, *How God Changes Your Brain: Breakthrough Findings from a Leading Neuroscientist* (New York: Ballantine Books, 2009), 19–20.

7. Goulston, *Just Listen*, 17.

8. Even hippocampal-managed memories will have biases and imperfections. Research has repeatedly demonstrated that, even though we would all strongly deny it, our memories are tinged with bias of previous exposures. In addition, each time we reexamine a memory, it is subject to alterations, edits, and redactions. Despite this, as our memory of an event changes over the years, we remain confident that our recollection is the same today as it was in the past. If you're like me, even now you may be thinking, *Yes, that is true of others. But I am confident in what I remember.* Thus, we should have some level of humility when we recall any memories.

## Chapter 7: Write a New Plot

1. Frederick Buechner, *Telling Secrets* (San Francisco: HarperSanFrancisco, 1991), 30.

2. Daniel Taylor, *Tell Me a Story: The Life-Shaping Power of Our Stories* (St. Paul, MN: Bog Walk Press, 2005), 13.

## Chapter 8: Tell Your Story

1. Daniel Taylor, *Creating a Spiritual Legacy: How to Share Your Stories, Values, and Wisdom* (Grand Rapids, MI: Brazos Press, 2011), 9.

## Chapter 9: Expressive Writing

1. Jerry Sittser, *A Grace Disguised: How the Soul Grows Through Loss* (Grand Rapids, MI: Zondervan, 1995), 128.
2. Susan Nolen-Hoeksema, Blair E. Wisco, and Sonja Lyubomirsky, "Rethinking Rumination," *Perspectives on Psychological Science* 3, no. 5 (2008): 400–24.
3. Pennebaker's early landmark studies launched a wave of several hundred other psychological studies on expressive writing. This subsequent research demonstrated positive results from this type of processing and added more nuance and validation to Pennebaker's earlier conclusions. Pennebaker provides a fantastic summary of the expressive writing literature in his book, *Expressive Writing: Words That Heal* (Enumclaw, WA: Idyll Arbor, 2014).
4. Social scientist Ethan Kross has done important work to sort out why some expressive writing recipes are more helpful than others. In an important paper published in *Psychological Science*, Kross and his colleagues recognized that some people failed to receive any benefit from expressive writing. So they wondered, "How can individuals face negative emotions without being overwhelmed by them?" They then conducted two studies. The first demonstrated that when the writers captured their story from a "self-distanced" as opposed to a "self-immersed" perspective, they experienced more benefit. Similarly, when writers were directed to write from the perspective of "why did this happen" as opposed to simply "what happened," they experienced more benefit. Ethan Kross, Ozlem Ayduk, and Walter Mischel, "When Asking 'Why' Does Not Hurt:

Distinguishing Rumination from Reflective Processing of Negative Emotions," *Psychological Science* 16, no. 9 (2005): 709–15.

5. Miroslav Volf, *The End of Memory: Remembering Rightly in a Violent World* (Grand Rapids: MI: Eerdmans, 2006), 28.
6. The process of neural reorganization is thought to contribute to the therapeutic effects of EMDR for survivors of trauma (mentioned earlier on page 194).
7. Melissa M. Kelley, *Grief: Contemporary Theory and the Practice of Ministry* (Minneapolis: Fortress, 2010), 75.

## Chapter 10: Further Steps on the Journey

1. I love to read books on grief, forgiveness, and gratitude. For a list of my favorites, visit my website, www.scottvaudrey.com /resources. I've compiled a bibliography of the titles I've found most helpful, both in my own life and in coaching others.
2. Henry Cloud, *Changes That Heal: Four Practical Steps to a Happier, Healthier You* (Grand Rapids, MI: Zondervan, 2003), 84.
3. C. S. Lewis, *A Grief Observed* (San Francisco: HarperOne, 1961), 3.
4. Nayyirah Waheed, *Nejma* (Scotts Valley, CA: CreateSpace, 2014).
5. Melissa M. Kelley, *Grief: Contemporary Theory and the Practice of Ministry* (Minneapolis: Fortress, 2010), 134–35.
6. Karen J. Maroda, *Seduction, Surrender, and Transformation: Emotional Engagement in the Analytic Process* (El Dorado Hills, CA: Analytic Press, 1998), 16.
7. Paul W. Coleman, "The Process of Forgiveness in Marriage and the Family" in *Exploring Forgiveness*, ed. Robert D. Enright and Joanna North (Madison, WI: University of Wisconsin Press, 1998), 94.
8. To learn more about these widespread societal benefits, google the Truth and Reconciliation Project in South Africa and the Parents Circle Families Forum in Israel–Palestine.
9. While we don't need compensation or ownership to offer forgiveness, we may still require compensation to receive justice, and we'll still need ownership to achieve trust and reconciliation.

10. Cloud, *Changes That Heal*, 198.

11. Thomas Szasz, *The Second Sin* (Garden City, NY: Anchor Press, 1973), 51.

12. Mahatma Gandhi, *All Men Are Brothers: Life and Thoughts of Mahatma Gandhi, as Told in His Own Words* (New Delhi: Navajivan, 1995).

13. Robert A. Emmons and Michael E. McCullough, "Counting Blessings Versus Burdens: An Experimental Investigation of Gratitude and Subjective Well-Being in Daily Life," *Journal of Personality and Social Psychology* 84, no. 2 (2003): 377–89.

14. Robert A. Emmons, *Gratitude Works! A Twenty-One-Day Program for Creating Emotional Prosperity* (San Francisco: Jossey-Bass, 2013), 10.

15. When I lived in Illinois, one of my quirky mindfulness exercises involved walking along the Lake Michigan shore. The Great Lakes possess the greatest variety of rocks along their shores than anywhere else on earth. So on many Saturday mornings I drove to Lake Michigan to wander the shores and collect rocks that, beneath their surface, potentially possessed great beauty. Back home I put the rocks in a rock tumbler through five or six stages of polishing. Each stage tumbled 24/7 for seven to fourteen days, with a progressively finer grit and eventually a clear polish. Remember stones can be used as reminders to forgive others, pray for another, accept others, remember a lost one, have a more positive attitude, or, in my case, be grateful. I have been so helped by the practice of carrying these remember stones that nowadays I give my coaching clients their own remember stone to reinforce the work they have done. If you're a rock nerd like me or just curious, check out my website (www.scottvaudrey.com/rocks) for photos of some of my polished Lake Michigan rocks.

# About the Author

Scott Vaudrey is a retired emergency department doctor. He received his MD from the University of Washington in 1988, and MA in transformational leadership from Bethel University in 2005. After transitioning from medicine to ministry, he served as a pastor for sixteen years, helping people navigate their relational challenges. Today he splits his time between executive coaching and speaking to staff teams, businesses, and nonprofits around the country about how to improve relationships and create thriving team cultures. Scott and his wife, September, raised five children and have three grandkids. They live in Southern California.

To learn more, visit scottvaudrey.com.